The church should value *The*

a hugely helpful resource con

the advantage of developing a thorough understanding of missions by applying scriptures and biblical principles to front-line mission work deep in Papua's jungles. *The Missionary Crisis* correctly emphasizes the gospel's vital importance, the necessity of sound theology, the non-negotiable qualifications of the missionary's character and life, and the continuing care he should prioritize for his family. It should be read prayerfully by every missionary, pastor, and church member to understand and practice the vital work of missions biblically and effectively.

– Jamey Tucker | HeartCry Missionary Society
Asia Coordinator

Honestly, there should be no need for a book like this in the evangelical church. But the author's experience and ours proves that much of the church today, starting with pastors and missionaries, has abandoned the apostle Paul's approach to missions: "I determined not to know anything among you except Jesus Christ and Him crucified." So in an age where trust in God and His methods and His results has been replaced with the pragmatic inventions of men, this book appears as an honest, passionate call to all who would serve in the Lord's mission—preach the gospel to yourself, to your family, to your church, and to the world.

– Mark Reed | Pastor, Rosemont Baptist Church
Winston-Salem, NC

For too long have missionaries gone to foreign fields of service unprepared and with little accountability. Paul's book brings a fresh perspective to missionary life and family. He shines a beam on the various responsibilities of those whom the Lord calls to His harvest fields. It is a much-needed resource for missionaries, mission boards, and churches alike.

– Mark Snider | Pastor, Bethany Bible Church
Big Lake, MN

Paul Snider's book, *The Missionary Crisis,* is like looking through a window. He divulges the plight of modern missions with engaging reality. As a missionary, Paul's perspective will afford the reader a much greater concern for what is called today *kingdom advancement.* Years ago, a mission director said that "the mission field is littered with uncrucified flesh." His assessment, both then and now, is accurate. But Paul doesn't stop after exposing the encumbrances to global missions; he offers biblical and practical solutions to the problems. Local churches, mission agencies, and anyone with an interest in gospel mission enterprise will profit immensely from this superb work.

– **Don Currin | HeartCry Missionary Society**
Eastern European Coordinator

Paul Snider has served the people of Papua Indonesia faithfully, and he is now serving the global church as well with *The Missionary Crisis.* From the importance of personal piety to theological understanding to local church responsibility, Paul has outlined what plagues the modern missionary movement. If men will heed the truths this book highlights, more *and* better churches will be established around the globe. Missionaries, pastors, church leaders, and all who love the gospel should read and apply the realities that Paul explains from a biblical foundation.

– **Anthony Mathenia | Pastor, Christ Church**
Radford, VA

Paul Snider has given the church a corrective, instructive, and helpful book on missions. In fact, *The Missionary Crisis* is one of the most practical resources on the topic I have read. Snider not only warns against the many dangers currently plaguing missions and missionaries today but also provides the biblical corrective. According to Snider, healthy missions is rooted in healthy ecclesiology. Every church and every missionary needs to read this book. It will aid in shaping, or reshaping, how you think about the Great Commission.

– **Jeff Johnson | President, Grace Bible Theological Seminary**
Conway, AR

THE MISSIONARY CRISIS

THE
MISSIONARY
CRISIS

CASE: 3597349
MISSIONARY TO SOUTH AFRICA
SENDING CHURCH: U.S.A #4568

FIVE DANGERS
PLAGUING MISSIONS & HOW THE CHURCH
CAN BE THE SOLUTION

PAUL SNIDER

FREE
GRACE
PRESS

Published by
Free Grace Press
815 Exchange Ave., Ste. 101
Conway, AR 72032

email: support@freegracepress.com
website: www.freegracepress.com

Printed in the United States of America
First printing 2021; reprinted 2022

Cover design by Scott Schaller

ISBN: 978-1-952599-41-5

*For additional Reformed Baptist titles, please email us
for a free list or see our website at the above address.*

To

Patricia

my best friend and loving wife,

who has given up countless comforts for endless hardships to follow me to the ends of the earth for the proclamation of the gospel. I love you!

And to

Lane and **Marianne**

my children,

may your lives display the glorious gospel of Jesus Christ here and abroad, and may you be committed to the gospel, doctrine, prayer, and family. I love you!

In memory of a dear friend and
fellow missionary in the gospel

Joel Tiegreen
January 2, 1985—April 13, 2021

Joel, you have fought the fight, finished your race,
and kept the faith (2 Tim. 4:7).

Some of Joel's last words to me were "It's all of grace! The more I
reflect on my life and deeds, the more I see nothing good except
God. So thankful for Christ!"

Joel was a husband, father, and missionary of whom the world was
not worthy. He was a man who understood the gospel well, loved to
preach and teach the truth, loved the doctrines of Scripture, poured
himself out continually to God in prayer, submitted himself and his
ministry to the authority of the local church, and loved his family
dearly. Thank you, dear brother, for your example to follow as a
husband, father, and missionary. Until we meet in glory!

Contents

Foreword

The church has been commanded to go out into all the world and make disciples of every "tribe and language and people and nation" (Rev. 5:9, see also 7:9). This command comes from none other than the Lord Jesus Christ (Matt. 28:18–20) and must be fulfilled with the greatest diligence and care.

The Great Commission is a difficult task that is greatly opposed, not only by fallen and sinful men but also by the most powerful and malignant beings in creation. Paul writes, "For our struggle is not against flesh and blood, but against the rulers, against the powers, against the world forces of this darkness, against the spiritual forces of wickedness in the heavenly places" (Eph. 6:12, paraphrased).

The Great Commission is a complicated task. Every step required to select, send, and keep a missionary on the field requires great wisdom on the part of the sender and the one sent. The discerning of the call, the preparation, the ordination, the sending, and the sustaining are beyond the expertise or skill of men.

The Great Commission is a spiritual task. It cannot be accomplished by the wisdom or power of man but must be executed according to what is written and in the power of the Holy Spirit.

To navigate this challenging world of missions, the Word of God must be a lamp to our feet and a light to our path (see Ps. 119:105). To persevere on this most difficult of roads, we must be "clothed with power from on high" (Luke 24:49).

Paul Snider's work stands firmly on the aforementioned truths. After years of serving on one of the most spiritually and physically demanding mission fields in the world—the remote jungles of Papua, Indonesia—Paul has witnessed firsthand the impotence of human strategies and the feebleness of the human will. He knows by experience the great cost of carrying the gospel to the most remote parts of the globe. These credentials place him at a unique vantage point to evaluate both the strengths and weaknesses of modern missions. Borrowing from the author of Hebrews, we might say that he has a keen idea of how to strengthen the hands that are weak and the knees that are feeble and make straight paths (see Heb. 12:12–13) in which future missionaries and churches might walk together.

Although this book is not a theological treatise, it is sound in its theology and seeks to be faithful in its application. Even when Paul speaks from experience, the counsel he gives is grounded in the Scriptures. This is refreshing but all too uncommon in a day when so much of the church's ministry both at home and abroad is guided by the unfaithful compass of psychology, sociology, and pragmatism. But the most attractive aspect of this work exudes from every page: It is evident that Paul loves Christ, loves the gospel, loves the nations, loves missionaries (even the weakest), and loves the churches that send them.

This book is not a harsh commentary that highlights all the errors of modern missions and leaves it in a hopeless pile of ruin. Instead, it is an instructive manual that is designed to aid churches and missionaries as they navigate the difficult road of missions. For this reason, this book is helpful to all who labor in missions—the aspiring missionaries, the veterans, and the faithful churches that send them.

Paul Washer
Founder and Missions Director
HeartCry Missionary Society
2021

Preface

This book is not an appeal for more missionaries. Nor is it a plea for you to go and die for the gospel—that is the "easy" part of missions. This work does not discuss missiology. Instead, it addresses several dangers that are becoming more prevalent among missionaries, it speaks to the church and its role in the Great Commission, and it focuses on the greatest dangers that have arisen over the last decade on the missionary field and within the church.

In our day and age of sending missionaries, a crisis is happening that we do not recognize. The missionary movement in America in the last decade has seen a surge in its emphasis on the importance of sending and going. Across the country, multiple mission conferences spur people into action for cross-cultural work. Well-known books encourage radical decisions to carry the gospel to unreached peoples. Missiologists provide statistics, terms, and definitions that inspire us to be the first among a particular people group. Passionate pastors urge men and women to lay down their lives for the gospel.

These are all commendable endeavors, but in our quest to fan the flame for more missionaries, we are missing the target. A crisis in the overall sending and going is leaving many missionaries on the mission field unqualified and unprepared. We must address the hype we are experiencing in America regarding the missionary's preparation and the church's role. Too long has the church neglected, perhaps from simple ignorance, its responsibility to send the right people.

In our day, when many churches see someone desiring to pursue full-time missions, it is frequently left up to the individual to prepare on their own. Many churches sit back, content to write a check and read an update without investing in the missionary's life. When this happens, we as a church body have poor, immature, and unqualified missionaries laboring to do a work that was designed for mature, qualified, and prepared people. Missions is a divine work. Too many missionaries and churches do not take the Great Commission seriously, and the results are evident on the field.

Missionaries cannot pursue the Great Commission alone, or they will fail. Many who go it alone wither and die quickly because mission work was not designed to be a solo endeavor. Mission work was designed for partnership, and either the church allowed them to go to the field untested or the missionaries slipped through and found their own way to serve. The church is the primary functioning heartbeat in missions, and its partnership with missionaries in the execution of the Great Commission is essential.

The Crisis

With this imbalance and the lack of adequate partnership, training, and accountability between the church and those it sends to the field, we are observing a troubling trend of missionaries who do not know the gospel, do not place importance on biblical doctrine, do not recognize the significance of constant prayer, are drowning in a lack of accountability, and place missionary work above the family. What is the missionary to do? What is the church to do?

As believers in Christ Jesus, we must find the core of the problem and take every step to honor our Lord by repenting of our lackadaisical heart toward his mission for the world. We must regain a heart full of vigor for the purity of the gospel's proclamation. We must live our lives as if each breath depends on biblical doctrine. We must train a generation of missionaries that prioritizes sweet, divine communion with God in prayer and enters into it daily. We must facilitate and require a life of accountability for men and women on the field so they do not fall into condemnation. And we must restore the number one responsibility that God ordained for the missionary—the family.

All these things are attainable, but only if the church and the missionary see their importance through the lens of Scripture. In the following chapters, I address five crises plaguing the missionary and the church. The last chapter is specifically for the church and gives practical instruction for your missionary's well-being.

A Quick Word to the Missionary

As you read this book, my prayer is that you will examine your life to see if you are living in any of these dangers. I pray that you will not only learn from these pages but also seek to live a life that honors Christ by committing to know the gospel clearly through deep and passionate study, giving biblical doctrine its primary importance, living a life of prayer without which you will wither away, submitting to accountability so that you can live a life of service in holiness, and not placing your ministry above your family.

I pray that you will not approach this great work alone— you need your church. If the elders and members are distant and uninvolved in your ministry, take heart, exhort them in love, and show them what their role must be in your life and in the work of the gospel. I pray you find comfort and strength to press on in faithfulness to the Word of God until the end.

A Quick Word to the Church

My prayer for the church is that if you are not taking initiative to intentionally partner with your missionaries, you will approach them with new eyes. Missionaries cannot be left on their own to do this tremendous, taxing work. The Great Commission is about the local church and its command to preach the gospel to the nations. Your missionaries are an extension of you—no separation should exist between the missionary and the church.

I pray that you find this book a help and encouragement as you send missionaries to the most difficult places in the world. You are the means that Christ has graciously granted to extend his message to the ends of the earth. Be ready. Be vigilant to go into the fires with your missionary for the sake of the lost.

What Is a Missionary?

The word *mission* is birthed from the Latin word *mitto*, which means "to send." It refers to someone who is sent somewhere for a specific purpose. In Luke 10:2, Jesus uses the Greek verb *exballo* when he commands the seventy-two missionaries and the reader to pray that more laborers be sent out. This verb means "to be thrust out," or to be sent away for a specific task. It also means "to dispatch—to send away towards a designated goal or purpose."[1] This indicates that a missionary is dispatched or thrust out into the world to complete a task. That task is prescribed by our Lord in his Word. But how does the word *missionary* receive its biblical definition and prescriptive command? The noun *missionary* is never used in Scripture. Many men throughout the last century have sought to give it a biblically concrete definition to maintain a distinction for the mission of the church. Several texts provide clarity:

- Go therefore and make disciples of all nations, baptizing them in the name of the Father and of the Son and of the Holy Spirit, teaching them to observe all that I have commanded you. And behold, I am with you always, to the end of the age. (Matt. 28:19–20)
- Go into all the world and proclaim the gospel to the whole creation. (Mark 16:15)
- And that repentance for the forgiveness of sins should be proclaimed in his name to all nations,

---

1   *The Bible Sense Lexicon: Dataset Documentation*, s.v. "*exballo*," accessed March 2020, https://ref.ly/logos4/Senses?KeyId=ws.dispatch.v.01.

beginning from Jerusalem. You are witnesses of these things. (Luke 24:47–48)

- As you sent me into the world, so I have sent them into the world. (John 17:18)
- But you will receive power when the Holy Spirit has come upon you, and you will be my witnesses in Jerusalem and in all Judea and Samaria, and to the end of the earth. (Acts 1:8)
- Therefore, we are ambassadors for Christ, God making his appeal through us. (2 Cor. 5:20)

All these passages speak of a charge to "be sent" to the spiritually dead sinner to proclaim repentance and faith in Jesus Christ. This is why they are referred to as "the Great Commission texts."

We see the first missionaries sent out by our Lord in Luke 10:2–3: "The harvest is plentiful, but the laborers are few. Therefore pray earnestly to the Lord of the harvest to send out laborers into his harvest. Go your way; behold, I am sending you out as lambs in the midst of wolves." The Lord appointed and sent these men to preach the good news. This is a missionary: one appointed for the proclamation of the gospel in a place that has no gospel. A missionary is a laborer for the Lord Jesus Christ sent to people who have not placed their faith in him alone.

Does this mean that everyone is a missionary? If everyone were a missionary, why would Jesus say "the laborers are few" (Luke 10:2)? Not everyone is a missionary. Everyone is a witness in his/her own geographical setting, but a missionary is someone who crosses over into a different culture, language, and political structure. A missionary is appointed to do a specific task for God's kingdom in a different cultural setting that has no gospel message. This does not mean that a person is a missionary simply because they engage in door-to-door evangelism or set up a community meal and preach the gospel in their own cultural setting. A missionary is a person confirmed by the local church to enter the full-time, long-term, cross-cultural work of preaching and teaching the gospel. In his book, *Reaching and Teaching: A Call to Great Commission Obedience*, M. David Sills says, "A proper definition of the term *missionary* distinguishes the missionary from an evangelist or preacher by including the idea of crossing boundaries for the sake of the gospel."[2] This definition keeps us from the error of making everything in the Christian life into missions. Although we should never minimize gospel work in any location (it is all of equal importance), we must distinguish what it means to be a missionary to fulfill Christ's command to "thrust out" missionaries to all nations.

Here is my working definition of a missionary: A missionary is a man who meets the qualifications of an elder or a woman who meets the qualifications of a deacon set by our Lord in Scripture and who is thrust out (*exballo*) for long-term service as a messenger by a local church into full-time, cross-cultural work, crossing ethnolinguistic boundaries to obey God's active command to preach the good news of Jesus Christ and disciple new believers in every nation until his second coming.

Therefore, as you read your way through these chapters, my prayer has already been that you will take Christ's command seriously: "Go therefore and make disciples of all nations, baptizing them in the name of the Father and of the Son and of the Holy Spirit, teaching them to observe all that I have commanded you. And behold, I am with you always, to the end of the age" (Matt. 28:19–20). A missionary is sent to do serious work and therefore must know the gospel of Jesus Christ to "make disciples."

---

2   M. David Sills, *Reaching and Teaching: A Call to Great Commission Obedience*, new ed. (Chicago: Moody, 2010), 92.

1

Missionaries Must
Understand the Gospel

I remember my first year in Indonesia like it was yesterday. The passion to learn the language, understand the culture, and preach the gospel in the local dialect burned in my heart. Excitement flowed from my soul as my family and I made a new life in a foreign land with the hopes of moving from language school to one of the remotest tribes in the world. Our first year was filled with its share of difficulties but none so hurtful and saddening as what I am about to share with you.

Twice a week after language class, a group of missionaries would meet to play basketball at a university just down the hill from our houses. Several well-known mission organizations were represented, and Westerners, Indonesians, Koreans, and Australians comprised the teams for these pickup games. These afternoons were a great opportunity for me to practice what I had learned in class with my Indonesian friends, who were mostly Muslims. This particular day still burns in my mind a decade later.

After one game, I was chatting with a Muslim friend.[1] He asked me pointedly what I was doing in Indonesia. My heart beat faster, drumming in my throat as I answered, "I am here to learn the language for a year, and then we will be moving to Papua to tell people about Jesus." Then I blurted out, "Have you heard of Jesus?"

One of my good friends, who was also a missionary learning the language and my next-door neighbor at the time, overheard me. Eagerly, he joined our conversation. Little did we know that one of the guys with us, a missionary from a well-respected American mission organization, heard us mention Jesus to this Muslim in the middle of the court. "Hey, you guys cannot mention the name of Jesus here like that," he whispered.

I stared at him. Had he really just said what I thought I heard? "What do you mean?" I asked.

"You cannot openly mention the name of Jesus here," he answered. "They do not know why we are here, and we could get kicked out of Indonesia."

My heart sank. Gesturing to the people around me, I replied, "These Indonesians know why we are here. They know we are Christians. The gospel came to this city in the 1950s—they know missionaries still come to this city."

He glared at me but said nothing.

I continued. "I will not stay silent about Jesus. That is why I was sent here."

We ended the conversation and went on to play a few more games. As we played, I could not help thinking about what had just happened. This man—a fellow missionary—was sent by a church body and a well-known mission organization, and yet he would not mention the name of Jesus for fear of being kicked out of the country. The next day, both my name and my friend's name were turned in to this mission organization's

---

1   In that first year in Indonesia, I learned that most Indonesians identify as "KTP Muslims," which means they are only classified as Muslims on their driver's licenses.

office for speaking the name of Jesus. We were considered dangerous and were to be avoided at all costs.

That example shows the argument many missionaries and mission organizations use: to live in a Muslim country, missionaries cannot speak the name of Jesus; preach the gospel openly; or use the titles of Christian, pastor, or missionary. Is this right?

Not Ashamed of the Gospel

It is dangerous to openly speak of Christ in some places. Their concerns are legitimate. In Indonesia, for example, it is against the law to proselytize anyone. Christians here have been arrested and sentenced to many years in prison for witnessing to Muslims. For this reason, many missionaries in Asia are "underground," meaning they do not draw attention to themselves with any communicative language that would expose who they are and why they are there. Conditions like these have led to new approaches to missions. One popular example is known as the C-Scale.

The C-Scale is a contextualization model for various approaches to get conversions to Christ. It teaches six different ways missionaries and indigenous Christians can draw nonbelievers to Christ while maintaining a culturally appropriate sensitivity to their ethnic identity. The problem with this approach is that it has caused many missionaries to change the way they do gospel work and has led to mistakes such as diminishing the truth, mixing other religions' beliefs with the gospel, accepting Muhammad and Jesus together, and avoiding the name of Christ.[2]

It is possible to overcontextualize to the point that we are no longer sharing the true gospel of Jesus Christ. We must exercise wisdom with caution. For example, I could not live in

---

2   For more information on the C-Scale, see Doug Coleman, *A Theological Analysis of the Insider Movement Paradigm from Four Perspectives: Theology of Religions, Revelation, Soteriology and Ecclesiology*, Evangelical Missiological Society Dissertation Series (Pasadena, CA: William Carey International University Press, 2011).

Aceh, Sumatra, Indonesia, under a visa that says "pastor" or "missionary." In some places in the world discretion and caution are needed to serve as a missionary. Many locations are dangerous, and wisdom is needed for when, where, and how we proclaim the gospel. It would be great stupidity on my part if I stood on a busy street corner in Sumatra and preached the gospel with a loudspeaker. My ministry would be over in just a few minutes. Many missionaries live without the titles and use wisdom in their ministry to stay long-term in their countries of service. No one should fault them for this.

"What about the danger you are placing on the nationals?" you might ask. Whenever the gospel is proclaimed in Muslim countries, danger will be present for both the missionary and the nationals. I know several Indonesians who converted to Christ and then had to flee their homes. One woman had a contract placed on her life. One man had his legs broken because he became a Christian. This is reality, but it should never stop a missionary from proclaiming the gospel. I would rather see nationals come to Christ and be persecuted for their faith than spend an eternity in hell separated from God. We must preach Christ and him crucified, no matter the cost (1 Cor 1:23).

Because multiple passages of Scripture prove that the name of Jesus must be proclaimed for salvation and is the only name to be spoken for salvation (Matt. 1:21; Acts 4:12; Rom. 10:13; Phil. 2:10), we must profess him with boldness. We cannot be so fearful that we allow man to control our mission, but we also must use Spirit-guided wisdom in our missionary endeavors.

So, what are missionaries to do in preaching Christ to dangerous people groups, especially where it is forbidden? What does Scripture teach us about preaching Christ in hostile places?

In Matthew 10:16 we learn a key principle: "Behold, I am sending you out as sheep in the midst of wolves, so be wise as serpents and innocent as doves." The wolf is powerful, and the sheep is weak, meaning the sheep will face danger. Yet Jesus said, "Be wise as serpents and innocent as doves." So, are we to keep our mouths closed and our Christianity private so as not to bring persecution or suffering on ourselves? Or are we to force our Christianity on others wherever we are, whatever we are doing, or whatever the time may bring? The answer to both questions is no. Instead, there must be biblical balance.

We should exercise caution with common sense but should not let that lead to laziness. Yes, we need to take care of ourselves, but the point this verse is making is that we must never allow the danger in missions to keep us from our duties for gospel preaching because we think only of safety. Many missionaries are unwilling to move forward in gospel proclamation simply because they do not want to face the danger and its consequences. Jesus commands us to move forward but with common sense like a serpent and simplicity like a dove.

On the basketball court, was it the proper time and place for me to speak of Jesus? Absolutely. It was not unwise of me to tell my Muslim friend about Jesus in this context. What would have been unwise is if I had gone to the local mosque and started preaching the gospel there. I would have been deported or jailed. We understand from Matthew 10:16 that we are to consider the place, time, and circumstances; we are not called to rush into danger without wisdom. But this should never quiet our souls or mouths for Christ's sake in hostile places.

I often feel great sadness for my Muslim basketball friends because I would give anything to see them repent and believe in the gospel. But how are they to repent and believe if no one speaks his name? How are they to come to know the Savior if we stay silent about the truth? Should we not proclaim Christ with all zealousness? What is happening to Christians in missions? When did it become normal in our missionary efforts to stay silent about the name of Jesus? What has happened to cause churches and organizations to send people who do not mention his name or wait years to do so? When did it become normal for one missionary to scold another for speaking about Jesus?

I believe that many missionaries (not all, because I know some great men and women who are not ashamed of Jesus) do not understand the gospel of Jesus Christ. That is why they do not preach to people, why they do not speak his name, and why this horrible trend is engulfing much of missionary sending. They simply do not understand the gospel the way Jesus did.

Although I am in no way patting myself on the back or claiming I have an understanding no one else has, I am saying that, as messengers of the gospel, it is essential we know it backward and forward the way our Lord Jesus does. R. C. Sproul posited, "All of us have error mixed in with truth in our faith."[3] Yet we must strive to erase that error with a biblical understanding of the gospel.

From what I have witnessed on the field this last decade, many missionaries are being sent by churches and mission organizations without understanding the gospel message. They drift to the side of error and say nothing about the Christ who saved them, or they dilute the gospel's pure truth and "good report" with new and trendy formulas so as not to offend anyone or lose friends. Did the missionary who scolded me for talking about Jesus understand the gospel? Sadly, no, because if he had truly grasped its message, he would not have remained silent.

The gospel does not call for the avoidance of Christ's name. It is the greatest message in the world; therefore, Jesus is the greatest message in the world. Sadly, many missionaries have the idea that speaking Christ's name should be prohibited in order to make and keep friends or to remain in the country. I am tired of the lack of gospel clarity on the mission field. Later in this chapter, I will present a few solutions and discuss how we can overcome gospel ignorance.

---

3   R. C. Sproul, "Questions & Answers," Standing Firm: 2012 West Coast Conference (Sanford, FL: Ligonier, 2012), http://www.ligonier.org/learn/conferences/standing-firm-2012-west-conference/questions-and-answers-west-conference.

The Message of the Gospel Is Worth Losing Our Lives

How I have longed to put the gospel into words, to explain and defend its truth. Long ago, I made a commitment that if I ever wrote a book on any mission topic, I would start with the most beautiful, awesome, and captivating story ever told: the gospel.

That is how we should start anything in life. The gospel made us a new creation in Christ (2 Cor. 5:17), so that means every breath, every thought, and every moment is made to glorify Jesus in gospel thought and gospel action (1 Cor. 10:31). There is nothing outside the gospel.

Many other books have explained the gospel in biblical and theological detail. But I am writing this for the missionaries preparing to go and those already on the field. I hope many others such as church members, church leaders, and mission organizations will take this book to heart and implement the steps necessary to prepare and send out men and women who truly understand the gospel (1 Tim. 4:6).

As believers and even more so as missionaries preparing to preach the gospel, it is imperative that we understand this message of Jesus Christ. We must proclaim him and his life, death, resurrection, and ascension with clarity. We must preach it passionately and with understanding so that people dead in their sin will be made alive through the Holy Spirit. If we ourselves do not understand this, then we have no business being on the mission field.

I am not talking about understanding the Four Spiritual Laws, the Romans Road method, or a sinner's prayer ideology.[4]

---

4 The Four Spiritual Laws are four guided statements, accompanied by Scripture, that believers can share with unbelievers to lead them to Christ. They include truths about humanity's separation from God and that Jesus is the only way we can be saved. After the four laws are explained, believers are to encourage unbelievers to pray. Bill Bright, founder of Campus Crusade for Christ (now CRU in the United States) wrote these four laws as a short booklet in the 1950s, see Bill Bright, "Have You Heard of the Four Spiritual Laws?" CRU Press, https://crustore.org/catalog/product/view/id/918/s/4-spiritual-laws-english/category/150. The Romans Road method is an approach that moves through verses in Romans with statements such as "We are all sinners by nature and by choice"

I am talking about understanding the gospel the way our Lord Jesus understood it and proclaimed it. As missionaries, you and I must labor to know and understand the gospel to the point that we are ready to lose our lives for it. I believe it is more important than our well-being and comfort.

Jesus is the best and only example worth speaking about concerning losing our lives for the gospel. John 1:14 tells us, "And the Word became flesh and dwelt among us, and we have seen his glory, glory as of the only Son from the Father, full of grace and truth." From this beautiful little verse, we learn several truths concerning Jesus's life.

First, we see the word *flesh*. Indeed, this second person of the Trinity became a man. He is truly God and truly man. The Greek word for "flesh" is *sarx*, which teaches that Jesus had a physical, functioning body with the same skin that covers our bones. He felt emotion, pain, happiness, and sadness. He is a living being in the flesh.

Second, this verse says Jesus "dwelt among us." This is the Greek root word *skene*, meaning "tent" or "tabernacle." Jesus became a physical body to take up a home with us, to live with us, and to make his habitat earth where sinful people live. The Son of God became a man and lived with haters of God to glorify his Father. He did this by being obedient to do his Father's will (John 6:38).

My mind goes right to this question: Is Jesus's life more valuable than ours? Yes! It absolutely is because he is God. "By him all things were created" (Col. 1:16). He is the one who "was in the beginning with God" (John 1:2). "He upholds the universe by the word of his power" (Heb. 1:3). This is the

---

(Rom. 3:23); "We receive eternal life as a free gift" (Rom. 6:23); "God demonstrated his love for us, his enemies" (Rom. 5:8); "We must trust and surrender to Jesus as Lord" (Rom. 10:9–10); and "Our assurance of salvation is through Jesus" (Rom. 10:13). This article explains the Romans Road method in depth: https://www.crosswalk.com/faith/spiritual-life/what-is-the-romans-road-to-salvation-bible-verses-and-meaning.html. For an explanation of the sinner's prayer, see Paul Washer, *Ten Indictments against the Modern Church*, Reformation Today Series (Grand Rapids: Reformation Heritage Books, 2018).

one who "committed no sin, neither was deceit found in his mouth" (1 Peter 2:22).

He is the most valuable person in eternity, so why did Jesus not worry about his well-being or comfort? After all, he is King of Kings. Why was he so ready and willing to lose his life for sinful men? The reason is this: he thought not of himself but of pleasing and obeying his Father (Ps. 40:8; John 6:38). He glorified his Father by obeying his Father's will, which was living a life as a human being, preaching the gospel, and enduring the humiliation of the cross. He was ready to lose his life so that sinners might repent and believe and have everlasting life (Matt. 20:28; Mark 1:15).

It was not the cross alone that glorified his Father, as wonderful as that is to us, but also his life as a man (the God-man), a life filled with suffering. We know this because of John 17:5: "And now, Father, glorify me in your own presence with the glory that I had with you before the world existed." To leave a perfect, beautiful, divine, holy home and come to live in a filthy, rotten, dark, sinful one would be objectionable. It would be depressing for you and me. In fact, human beings would not blink an eye at deserting such conditions—we would leave as quickly as we could.

But Jesus did not leave or say to his Father, "I cannot stay in this kind of place; bring me home." He stayed as the perfect man. He had no place to lay his head (Luke 9:58). He suffered insult after insult (Isa. 53:7), weakness in his body (John 4:6), multiple attempts on his life (John 5:18), rejection from his own people (Luke 4:24), and finally, beatings and death (Luke 22:63; Acts 3:15). Jesus knew what it felt like and what it meant to be a sinner but without sin (2 Cor. 5:21). He never disobeyed, never stopped preaching the truth, and never left despite the hateful conditions here on earth. This is the ultimate example that we as missionaries have in living and losing our lives for our Lord Jesus.

If we remain silent about him and instruct others to do so, we dishonor our Savior and what he died for and have an unbiblical understanding of the gospel contrary to that of Jesus in his earthly ministry. Truthfully, we do not have the gospel. The gospel is not silent. It is active, not passive.

Some missionaries go to difficult places. The problem is what they do *not* preach or speak of in those places. I know the thinking of many missionaries—they believe our Lord is pleased with them because they chose a difficult place to serve. Therefore, they feel justified with their decisions not to speak of Jesus at a particular time. But God is no more pleased with you for going to those hard places than he is pleased with you *positionally* in Christ Jesus. We cannot make Jesus Christ any happier with us or make him love us any more just because we do something radical by going to a dangerous place.

In Christ, you and I are loved as much as we ever will be because of his substitutionary atoning work, not because of any work we have done. Even in these hard places and different cultures, we should pack up and go home if we think like the missionary who told me to remain silent instead of speaking about Jesus. If all missionaries understood the gospel the way Scripture teaches and the way Jesus preached it, then we would not be dissuaded even if we were amid the worst suffering imaginable. We would herald what the apostle Paul said: "Even if I am to be poured out as a drink offering upon the sacrificial offering of your faith, I am glad and rejoice with you all" (Phil. 2:17). We would offer our lives if necessary for the gospel advance. I have seen national Christians give their lives for the proclamation of the gospel. They cared not for themselves but only for what gave them true joy even during severe persecution and discomfort—Christ. This humbles and challenges me to stay the course and follow Paul's words in Philippians 2:17.

In his book *Reckless Abandon*, my friend David Sitton says, "Risk assumes the possibility of loss and is always determined by the value of the mission. The gospel is so valuable that no risk is unreasonable. Life is gained by laying it down for the gospel. If I live, I win and get to keep on preaching Christ. If I die, I win bigger by going directly to be with Christ and I get to take a few tribes with me."[5] Even when missionaries die for gospel preaching, they do not lose their lives but save them. The nationals who come to Christ also receive their reward, which is far greater than any earthly gain. Mark 8:35 says, "For whoever would save his life will lose it, but whoever loses his life for my sake and the gospel's will save it."

As missionaries, we have the greatest, most important work in the world. The King of the Universe has chosen us out of multitudes to be his ambassadors. He tasks us with proclaiming his message. How could it be that the holiest, most righteous, and only God would choose to send you and me? Therefore, we must strive hard to know the gospel because when we know the gospel Jesus preached, we will find ourselves, by the Holy Spirit's help, preaching Christ in places where other people would not dare speak.

Maybe you are a missionary already on the field; maybe you are guilty of not speaking his name. Maybe you are operating under a belief system that teaches missionaries to wait until they feel ready or when their organization tells them to because of some teaching method. I have seen it firsthand on the mission field. These are real crises.

What should we do? Flee to Christ. Fall on his mercy. Repent of our ignorance of the gospel and go to Scripture and study. Let the Holy Spirit take what he shows us from the Bible and use that to lose our lives for his sake.

The Gospel

How should we start preaching the gospel to individuals or crowds? Whether we are with a friend on the basketball court, a crowd of Muslims in a large city, or a tribe in the jungles of Papua, the message is the same. What is this message and what should we know about it? As messengers, how should we proclaim it?

---

5   David Sitton, *Reckless Abandon: A Modern-Day Gospel Pioneer's Exploits Among the Most Difficult to Reach Peoples* (Greenville, SC: Ambassador International, 2013), 22.

To answer these questions, we first must know the answer to the question, What is the gospel? The gospel is not something we "share" or "tell." That kind of language permeates the evangelical world today. Rather, the gospel is something we preach. It is a message we proclaim to the spiritually dead sinner. When we explain the gospel and all its parts, we must not use that kind of watered-down language. We preach. We proclaim in life or in death.

What is the gospel? The word *gospel* is from the Greek word *euangelion* and means good news, glad tidings, or good report. The good news is a proclamation of something that is good for its hearers. The gospel is the good news about the person and work of Jesus Christ. That proclamation is the good news about Jesus's life, death, burial, resurrection, and ascension. The good news is a proclamation that through Jesus's life, death, and resurrection human beings can have peace with God through repentance of sin and belief in the work of Christ by faith.

In Romans 1:16, Paul tells us that the gospel "is the power of God for salvation to everyone who believes, to the Jew first and also to the Greek." The good news is a proclamation of God's power giving salvation to spiritually dead human beings through Christ. The good news is a proclamation to be saved from something into something. The good news is God the Father sending his only Son to give eternal life to those who repent of sin and believe on his name. Christ becomes ours and we become his. The good news is that he gladly forgives the sin of man and breaks down the dividing wall of hostility between man and God (Eph. 2:14).

The bad news is that all human beings are rebels. We are haters of God. We are not righteous. We are not holy. We love our own sin. We love the darkness rather than the light (John 3:19). We are evil to the core. We are born in sin (Ps. 51:5). We do not want God nor seek him out (Ps. 14:1–3). In other words, we are spiritually dead. We are dead in our trespasses and sins (Eph. 2:1). Spiritually speaking, we are corpses that cannot and will not obey God. We are wicked human beings (Jer. 17:9).

Why? Because we are like our first father, Adam, who disobeyed God's law. God said, "But of the tree of the knowledge of good and evil you shall not eat, for in the day that you eat of it you shall surely die" (Gen. 2:17). Because of that one act of disobedience, death spread to all men (Rom. 5:12). Therefore, because you and I are from Adam, we sin by nature. Everything we do is from a sinful heart. No one is guiltless before God.

In his book *The Gospel of Jesus Christ*, Paul Washer writes, "Before he fell into sin, man's original state was noble, but man's present condition is desperate. The Bible teaches us that although humankind was created good (Genesis 1:26, 31), all humans have fallen into spiritual death (Ephesians 2:1). We are by nature morally corrupt, inclined toward evil, and hostile toward the righteous God."[6]

God is full of indignation, and his wrath hangs over each sinner. At any moment he chooses, he can unleash his full fury on sinners and cast them into hell, "where their worm does not die and the fire is not quenched" (Mark 9:48). But through Christ's life, death, and resurrection, we have access to God, whereas before we were closed off to him. We were enemies of God. We could not be near God or be in His presence because of our sin.

But through Christ's substitutionary atonement (meaning Christ took our place), he willingly accepted the wrath of his Father that we deserved. The punishment should have been ours, but Christ obediently endured it. He brought us back to God. He reconciled us to God (Rom. 5:10; 2 Cor. 5:18). We are no longer rebels. We have the forgiveness of sins in the person and work of Christ. We are saved by his life (2 Tim. 1:9). Jesus Christ obediently and willingly suffered the torture of the cross (Isa. 53:7). He was beaten and crucified on a tree to bear the wrath of his Father (Rom. 5:9). He died so we may

---

6   Paul Washer, *The Gospel of Jesus Christ* (Grand Rapids: Reformation Heritage Books, 2016), 5.

have life that is everlasting, a life that is eternal the moment the Spirit's regenerative work begins in our hearts.

Christ's Life

The good news is that salvation has come in the incarnation of Jesus Christ. Jesus being the God-man has come to this earth making himself of no reputation, "but emptied himself, by taking the form of a servant, being born in the likeness of men. And being found in human form, he humbled himself by becoming obedient to the point of death, even death on a cross" (Phil. 2:7–8). Jesus came "not to be served but to serve, and to give his life as a ransom for many" (Mark 10:45).

In his book *Gospel Wakefulness*, Jared Wilson writes, "The good news is news about something that actually, literally happened in real life."[7] The reality is that for sinners this really did happen. It is objective truth, not some fairy tale or fantasy novel. This is news about the real life of a man who is perfect in his person. He is impeccable, and because of his impeccability he can command his creation to obey his words. The good news proclaims that this Christ lived a perfect, sinless life on earth. Jesus Christ is the epitome of all that is righteous, all that is holy, all that is just, and all that is good and pleasing. His life was anointed by the Spirit to proclaim himself as the salvation for the poor, the captives, and the oppressed (Luke 4:18).

The good news is about a command for us to obey. Christ's life demands it. The gospel is commanding us. Many missionaries are guilty of forgetting that the gospel is a command for the sinner, not a suggestion, wish, or guided prayer. When was the last time you used this kind of language in your gospel efforts? When was the last time you preached that this is a command? We must not be guilty of watering down the good news with liberalism, which tolerates a shallow proclamation whereby sinners do not understand the command of repentance given by our Lord Jesus. Jesus has all authority and every right as King to command people to repent and believe. Why? First, he is God. Second, he lived a perfect, sinless life on earth.

---

7   Jared C. Wilson, *Gospel Wakefulness* (Wheaton, IL: Crossway, 2011), 22.

The good news commands a response. The response calls for a positive reply. The good news is a command to repent and believe in Jesus Christ himself for the forgiveness of sins (Mark 1:15). We do not have to go any further than the four Gospels to see the perfect life of Jesus.

Jesus was born of a virgin by the Holy Spirit (Matt. 1:23; Luke 2:7). He became flesh, an ordinary man, and he made his home with us (John 1:14). Jesus is the *theanthropic* person, which means he embodies deity in human form. He grew up as a boy filled with wisdom (Luke 2:40) and continued to grow in wisdom and years, reaching great favor with God and man (Luke 2:52).

What is even more miraculous is that Jesus never sinned. In fact, Jesus is beyond sinless. In my humanity, I cannot fathom this. We must preach this point clearly: he never sinned. Not once did he disobey his mother. Not once did he lie to his Father. Not once did he have an impure thought. Not once did he have a proud heart. Let us look at several texts that verify this:

- For we do not have a high priest who is unable to sympathize with our weaknesses, but one who in every respect has been tempted as we are, yet without sin. (Heb. 4:15)
- For our sake he made him to be sin who knew no sin, so that in him we might become the righteousness of God. (2 Cor. 5:21)
- For God has done what the law, weakened by the flesh, could not do. By sending his own Son in the likeness of sinful flesh and for sin, he condemned sin in the flesh. (Rom. 8:3)
- He committed no sin, neither was deceit found in his mouth. (1 Peter 2:22)

If Jesus had sinned, then we are still in our sins and have no hope. This is what makes the gospel good news and beautiful for the sinner. Human beings have a sinless Christ on which to place all their sins, which were nailed to the tree (1 Peter 2:24). We must tell sinners this. Christ in his humanity did not sin. Bruce Ware gives insight to this beautiful doctrine when he says, "Jesus did not sin, not because he relied on his supernatural power of his divine nature or because his divine nature overpowered his human nature, keeping him from sinning, but because he utilized all of the resources given to him in his humanity."[8] We must preach the life of Christ in our gospel endeavors because without his life there is no gospel.

Christ's Death

Every missionary must preach Jesus's substitutionary atonement with such clarity that the sinner knows without a shadow of a doubt that Jesus is not to be refused. What is substitutionary atonement?

Christ's substitutionary atonement is this: He took our place in the eternal death we deserve when he offered himself up on the tree. Every sin (past, present, and future) was placed upon him as he suffered in body and soul, hanging on the cross. "He himself bore our sins in his body on the tree, that we might die to sin and live to righteousness" (1 Peter 2:24). This makes him our sacrificial lamb (John 1:29).

The efficacy of Christ's death is central to the gospel proclamation. I want every missionary to know this: The atonement is at the heart of the gospel. Christ's atoning death is an infinite atonement. Why? Jesus had to be truly God and truly man to be the payment for sin. He had to satisfy the wrath of a holy, infinite God. Being truly God, Jesus could offer up full payment to his Father whereby the Father would be pleased to accept it. Without his death on the cross, we would pay for our sins for eternity.

What makes it truly infinite is that he is truly God. However, Jesus paid for the sins of all the people the Father chose before the foundation of the world because he was truly man.

---

8   Bruce Ware, *The Man Christ Jesus: Theological Reflections on the Humanity of Christ* (Wheaton, IL: Crossway, 2013), 84.

There can be no substitution without a living, sinless sacrifice. Jesus satisfied the wrath of his Father so that we would have life everlasting and in turn worship him forever.

Jesus suffered and died for our sins so that we can know the Father and be in union with him (Isa. 53:4–6; 1 Peter 3:18). Sinners that have repented and trusted in the work of Christ by faith are declared not guilty before the judgment bar of the Father. This is what is known as our justification (Rom. 5:1). We are declared righteous.

As missionaries, we must understand the doctrine of justification. Do those we preach to know about God's judgment? Do they know they are guilty and deserving of death? Do they know that they can be found not guilty through the atoning death of Christ if they believe in him by faith? Do they know there is mercy for those who seek him, and justice for those who refuse him? We must preach this clearly with full conviction that what he did for us, he will do for them. If we do not, we have not only robbed God the glory due him, but we have also robbed the cross of its power and have not proclaimed the true gospel.

Paul Washer writes, "Christ did not die as a mere martyr, but as the Redeemer of sinful humanity. Before He breathed His last breath, He declared, 'It is finished!' (John 19:30). When He said this, He meant that through His suffering and death, He made full payment for the sins of those who believe in Him."[9] Justification is secured for us in the person and work of Christ when he declared "It is finished!" Because of that statement, those who repent and believe on Christ alone are declared not guilty. Isaiah 53:12 says that "he poured out his soul to death and was numbered with the transgressors; yet he bore the sin of many, and makes intercession for the transgressors."

No passage in Scripture better verifies Jesus's death, what it entailed, and the depths of it than John 10:14–15: "I am the good shepherd. I know my own and my own know me, just as the Father knows me and I know the Father; and I lay down my

---

9   Washer, *The Gospel of Jesus Christ*, 11.

life for the sheep." In verse 15, Jesus says, "I lay down my life." The words "lay down" (*tithemi*) are present active indicative, which means that Jesus in his humanity was in the process—at the present time in his ministry—of giving up something, setting aside his own rights and privileges. He was in the process of giving up himself for the people that will come to him. Jesus did not lay down his life just at the cross, even though that is the heartbeat of the gospel, but he was actively laying it down before he was nailed to the cross.

When Jesus said, "I am laying down my life," it is interesting that the word he uses is the Greek word *psyche*. Jesus does not use either of the two Greek words for "life" found in the New Testament but uses the Greek word for "soul." This word denotes that he is not just speaking about his physical body or his breath.[10] This word has to do with what is on the inside, the inner being of Jesus. What is it that suffers in Jesus to the point of death in his ministry to the cross? His soul: "He poured out his soul to death" (Isa. 53:12). Christ's soul was placed on the iron chair.[11] This is what makes him more beautiful than anything excellent. Every part of his soul was tormented and scourged because he bore our sin.

Wilhelmus à Brakel wrote, "The true cause of all His soul suffering was first of all that He felt the full extent of what sin is, as well as what it means to be a sinner."[12] Jesus endured

---

10   The first Greek word, *zoe*, means life in the physical sense or transcendent life (John 5:26; Acts 17:25; 1 Cor. 15:19; Heb. 7:3; Rev. 11:11). The second Greek word for "life" is *bios* and means life with all the activity, events, and affairs throughout its course (Luke 8:14; 1 Peter 4:3; 1 Tim. 2:2; 2 Tim. 2:4). See William Arndt, Frederick W. Danker, Walter Bauer, and F. Wilbur Gingrich, *A Greek-English Lexicon of the New Testament and Other Early Christian Literature* (Chicago: University of Chicago Press, 1979), 340.

11   The iron chair was an ancient torture device used to extract information. It was mostly used on criminals but was also employed on the accused. The person was strapped to a chair that was covered with iron spikes that punctured the skin, while hot coals were placed under the seat, roasting him alive. If he survived the extreme burns, the wounds from the spikes often caused multiple infections that ultimately led to death. See James McDonald, "Medieval Torture," Medieval Warfare, rev. February 24, 2015, https://www.medievalwarfare.info/torture.htm#chair.

12   Wilhelmus à Brakel, *The Christian's Reasonable Service* (Grand Rapids: Reformation Heritage Books, 1992), 1:579.

enormous physical suffering that no other man could have endured, but his soul suffered to death because the Father looked upon him as if he were the worst sinner to ever live, yet he was without sin. "Even as the Son of Man came not to be served but to serve, and to give his life [soul; *psyche*, Gr.] as a ransom for many" (Matt. 20:28).

This is important: Christ was not a sinner hanging on the cross. When every sin was placed on him, the Father viewed him as if he had committed all sin, although he was without sin. This is the beautiful doctrine of imputation. Sinners receive his righteousness and are completely cleared from the Father's judgment, and Jesus receives our sin and guilt and bears it unto death, to the point that his entire soul is in agony. Christ endured tremendous soul suffering. This is our Christ, the humble Son of Man who was "for a little while lower than the angels; you have crowned him with glory and honor, putting everything in subjection under his feet" (Heb. 2:7–8). Who would dare even to die for a good person, let alone die for a hater of God (Rom. 5:7–8)? This makes the preaching of Jesus's atoning death the centrality of the gospel.

Christ's Resurrection

In one of my cross-cultural training classes, the professor asked what most people forget in their preaching of the gospel. The room was silent. Finally, I raised my hand, and he looked at me expectantly. "Christians forget to preach the resurrection of Christ," I said. That was the answer he was looking for. Sadly, it is true. Gospel preachers often forget to place the importance of the resurrection in their gospel proclamations. But the resurrection is everything because it verifies the truth of who Jesus is. Frankly, there is no gospel message without the resurrection. It is the pinnacle of the good news.

What is the resurrection? In the New Testament, the Greek word *egeiro* is most used to denote Jesus's resurrection. It literally means "awaken." We know from Scripture that God awakened (raised) Jesus from the dead (1 Cor. 6:14). After Christ's vicarious death on the cross, the Scriptures teach us he was buried in a tomb (John 19:41–42) and raised on the third day (1 Cor. 15:4).

But why was Jesus raised? According to Romans 4:25, he was "raised for our justification." The verse also says, "who was delivered up for our trespasses." Jesus was executed first for our sin and then raised from the grave for our justification. In other words, everything that was done by Christ—"delivered up" and being "raised"—was done so that we would become righteous like him. It is finished! It is validated through Christ's resurrection. Everything concerning his resurrection is applied to us who believe. This makes sense because without his resurrection, we would be declared guilty before the Father. We would still be in our sins, condemned to suffer an endless death in torment, under the curse forever and ever, and separated from God. The apostle Paul placed Jesus's resurrection at the culminating point of the gospel. He writes, "If Christ has not been raised, then our preaching is in vain and your faith is in vain" (1 Cor. 15:14). As we preach the good news, the resurrection must flow from our mouths as if life depended on it. L. L. Morris writes, "Salvation is *not* something that takes place apart from the resurrection."[13] (Emphasis added.) The same power that awakened Jesus from the dead awakens sinners. This is the gospel.

The resurrection proves several points. First, it proves Jesus has power over sin and death (Acts 2:24). Second, it verifies that sinners can have new life (1 Peter 1:3). I explain to the Korowai people that when Jesus came out of the tomb, he showed all human beings that he has power over sin and death.[14] His was no ordinary returning from death. If it was

---

13   D. R. W. Wood, I. H. Marshall, A. R. Millard, J. I. Packer, and D. J. Wiseman, eds., *New Bible Dictionary*, s.v. "resurrection" (Morris, L. L), (Leicester, England; Downers Grove, IL: InterVarsity Press, 1996), 1012.

14   The Korowai tribe is a people group of about four thousand in the lowland swamps of Papua, Indonesia. They are known as the Treehouse People because they build their houses eight to ten meters above the ground. My family and I have been serving this people group for more than a decade. They are a seminomadic, animistic people who live to appease an evil spirit, Saip, through sacrificing pigs and other small animals and offering sago bread and various jungle foods on a sacred altar. When the fat and food is consumed, they believe Saip is pleased and

ordinary, like Lazarus's, then Jesus would be conditioned with the threat of death again. But according to Scripture, Jesus is the "firstfruits" from the dead (1 Cor. 15:20). This means he has an eternal resurrection. And by repentance and faith in his name, sinners too can share in this eternal resurrection, meaning, "He who raised Christ Jesus from the dead will also give life to your mortal bodies through his Spirit who dwells in you" (Rom. 8:11). Jesus himself said, "I am the resurrection and the life" (John 11:25). That is glorious news!

Third, Jesus's resurrection shows that the Father accepted the full payment for sin through his Son's death. Sin's power is broken and completely resolved in this exalting measure of Jesus's new life. Jesus destroyed sin through the power of his resurrection. Scripture testifies to this: "We were buried therefore with him by baptism into death, so that just as Christ was raised from the dead by the glory of the Father, we too might walk in newness of life" (Rom. 6:4). And God, "Even when we were dead in our trespasses, made us alive together with Christ—by grace you have been saved—and raised us up with him and seated us with him in the heavenly places in Christ Jesus" (Eph. 2:5–6).

R. C. Sproul unpacks this doctrine with great clarity: "Of course when He took our sin by imputation on the cross, He was filled with sin, but not His own. His inherent sinlessness denied death the authority to contain Him. So, it was not just *possible* for Jesus to rise again; it was *impossible* that He would *not* be raised from the dead. How can death hold a sinless human being? It cannot. So, Jesus was vindicated in the resurrection."[15] As missionaries, we must proclaim that through Christ's resurrection from the dead, God the Father is fully and

---

therefore will give them success in procreation and harvesting. They also worship sacred rocks, springs, and trees. The gospel came to the southern Korowai in the 1970s, but the northern Korowai were closed off until the early 2000s. Through the efforts of the Indonesian National Church in Papua and the missionaries, there are now a handful of believers. The northern Korowai tribe had no written language until 2018. The Salvation History Catechisms were completed and are now being used in the northern villages.

15   R. C. Sproul, *The Work of Christ: What the Events of Jesus' Life Mean for You* (Colorado Springs: David C Cook, 2012), 166.

truly happy with his Son's sacrifice. The Father has thrown into the farthest sea the curse for all who repent and believe (Mic. 7:19).

How do we combine all this and preach it? It takes study and work to proclaim the gospel clearly. In appendix A, I have compiled all I have written thus far concerning the gospel. I believe that as gospel messengers we should never start with the condition of man. We must always start our gospel preaching with the holiness of God. People must see their need for repentance weighed against a holy person, God himself. When we do that, we allow the sinner to see their sin in light of a holy and righteous God. They see their need for a savior. If we start with our current condition and leave God's holiness out of the message, then there is no backdrop against which to weigh their need. Do not forget, people love their sin (John 3:19). They must see the purity that reigns above them and compare themselves with that purity. Dr. Martyn Lloyd-Jones puts it beautifully:

> To fail to present the holiness of God is to strip the cross of Christ of its true meaning. It is the holiness of God that demands the cross, so without starting with holiness there is no meaning in the cross. It is not surprising that the cross has been discounted by modern theologians; it is because they have started with the love of God without His holiness. It is because they have forgotten the life of God, His holy life, that everything in Him is holy; with God love and forgiveness are not things of weakness or compromise. He can only forgive sin as He has dealt with it in His own holy manner, and that is what He did upon the cross.[16]

Dr. Lloyd-Jones has a beautiful understanding of the gospel. If God is not holy and righteous, then who has the power to forgive sin? We would use the same words as the apostle

---

16   Steven J. Lawson, *The Passionate Preaching of Martyn Lloyd-Jones* (Orlando: Reformation Trust, 2016), 116.

Paul and say, our "faith is in vain" (1 Cor. 15:14) if that were so. No missionary on the planet is able to preach the gospel in the power of the Holy Spirit unless he begins with the holiness of God. It is vital that we start with the character of God; otherwise, the gospel does not become a proclamation of good news for the sinner, but a proclamation of confusion and empty ideas. When we start with the holiness of God, the rest of truth's redemptive proclamation falls into majestic harmony.

We also preach the love of God. In any theological training, one of the first things we learn under the heading "Doctrine of God" is that beautiful attribute that he alone is love: "God is love" (1 John 4:8). "We love because he first loved us" (1 John 4:19). But why must we first divert to the love of God in our gospel preaching? Because it is seen and displayed in the glorious incarnation of his Son, Jesus Christ. Sure, God shows his love toward his creation in general everyday blessings, but the ultimate display of God's love is given to us in the person of Jesus Christ. God manifested that love in human form to die for sinners. Jesus Christ is the sacrifice for sin given to us by a loving Father who hates sin. Therefore, Christ is the perfect example of what love is to the human race:

- For God so loved the world, that he gave his only Son, that whoever believes in him should not perish but have eternal life. (John 3:16)
- Christ loved the church and gave himself up for her. (Eph. 5:25)
- For the Father himself loves you, because you have loved me and have believed that I came from God. (John 16:27)

Gospel Preaching

In conjunction with this chapter, a thorough example of how to preach the gospel to a people group that has yet to hear the name of Jesus is provided in full in Appendix A. This explanation will help you as missionaries to check each truth, proclaim the good news with clarity, and grow in your own life by the Spirit for gospel proclamation. This is not about us but about Jesus. We have nothing to say but what the Holy Spirit gives us.

That does not mean we do not prepare, but that we lay aside our wants and motives and pray that the Holy Spirit uses us as his messengers. If we have not already, we will face hostile individuals and crowds, but we cannot let this discourage us. We are sent by the King of Kings and are his ambassadors.

Sometimes people stare at me intimidatingly as quietness fills the room after I have preached the gospel. At various times I have seen fights break out and have been surrounded by multiple drunks while preaching. People stand up and scream at me and have disrupted the preaching because of what was said, and professing believers have hollered at me. One time, men rushed in with bows and arrows, and another time pigs ran in and disrupted the gospel message. Despite any obstacles we may face in our gospel preaching, we must not waver or grow weary. This is his gospel, and he will make sure it does not return void (Isa. 55:11).

The Gospel Message Begins in Genesis

If you are on the field and are teaching through each story of the Old and New Testament, I beg you not to wait until you reach the New Testament to preach the gospel. I have seen it all over the mission field. Many missionaries present Old Testament stories for several years and think the escalation of Jesus's story will surface once they enter the four Gospels. This is the wrong kind of methodology. Do not wait until you reach the New Testament to proclaim the person and work of Christ. Proclaim the gospel in every teaching session. The entire thirty-nine books of the Old Testament are about Christ Jesus. Many missionaries have accepted this false notion that to delay a gospel proclamation of Christ's person and work is valid for the people's understanding of how God worked in salvation history. Many mission organizations teach this.

But as messengers, we must proclaim the gospel in every teaching session. When you work your way from Genesis to Malachi, Christ is there, shining as beautiful as the sun. Every opportunity to teach a Bible story must have the gospel in it. Otherwise, what is the point of our ministry? If we wait to preach Christ until the New Testament, then we have robbed those people from seeing the glory of God. Let's not be guilty of waiting, maybe several years, to preach the good news. Preach it now. Seek the lost while they may be found. "We must work the works of him who sent me while it is day; night is coming, when no one can work" (John 9:4).

Father in heaven, help us, as your messengers to foreign lands, to understand the gospel of Jesus Christ and proclaim it with clarity by the power of your Spirit. Send out laborers who are equipped to handle your gospel with honor, even if it means loss of life or health. May we preach your gospel with full dependency on you and for your glory. Help us to study and proclaim the gospel of Jesus Christ with great passion, understanding, and boldness. Help us not to fear men but to joyfully reach the most dangerous places with your truth so that your name will be great among the nations. Amen.

2

No Doctrine, No Mission

We finished a year of language school in Java, and our first year in Papua, we built a house in the village of Danowage and settled into our remote life among the Korowai tribe. After six months of living in the village, we flew to a coastal town to resupply and attend a few national church meetings. Papuan church leaders and evangelists and several international missionaries were in attendance, and one missionary was to preach from the Word to encourage these Papuan men in their ministries.

Many of these tribes are extremely difficult places to serve, and most Papuan men have little training. It was a great opportunity to teach and encourage them in the Word. After opening in prayer, the missionary, who had been sent by a church in the States and a well-known mission organization, began to speak. If I could turn back time, I would erase the statement I heard from this missionary. I still cringe when I replay the moment in my mind. Looking around at the church leaders and evangelists serving throughout Papua, he stated, "Doctrine is not what you need right now."

I could not believe my ears. Did this missionary, sent to preach the gospel and co-labor with the Papuan church, which desperately needs solid doctrine, really just say that? I left that meeting feeling as if the enemy had won in the fight for biblical doctrine at its proper place in ministry. Would these Papuan men now consider the teachings of Scripture to be unimportant or "less than"? Would the teachings of Scripture ever make their debut as the most important truth these men could study? Would a toleration of other doctrines slip into this Papuan church and cause damaging results? An American church and mission organization had confirmed this missionary. How could this be?

Doctrine and Theology

Let me mitigate the confusion that permeates many missionaries' thoughts when it comes to this subject. What is biblical doctrine? Is it the same as biblical theology? You may have heard the words *doctrine* and *theology* used interchangeably, as if they are the same thing. This is a misconception. The word *doctrine* comes from the Latin word *doctrina*, meaning "teach." It also comes from the Greek New Testament words *didache* and *didaskalia*, meaning "the act or the content of teaching."[1] Even in the Old Testament we find the word *leqah* (concerning teaching), meaning "what is received."[2] The Hebrew word *tora*, meaning "law," is used 216 times in the Old Testament and refers to a group of publicized teachings.

The following are some passages of Scripture from the Old and New Testament showing the importance and priority of doctrine in the Christian life:

- May my teaching drop as the rain, my speech distill as the dew, like gentle rain upon the tender grass, and like showers upon the herb. (Deut. 32:2)

---

1   *The Bible Sense Lexicon*, s.v. "teaching," https://ref.ly/logos4/Senses?KeyId=ws.teaching.n.02.
2   Nixon, R. E., s.v. "doctrine," *New Bible Dictionary*, 280.

- For I give you good precepts; do not forsake my teaching. (Prov. 4:2)
- And they devoted themselves to the apostles' teaching and the fellowship, to the breaking of bread and the prayers. (Acts 2:42)
- But thanks be to God, that you who were once slaves of sin have become obedient from the heart to the standard of teaching to which you were committed. (Rom. 6:17)

How do we put all this together into a definition of doctrine? Here is my working definition: "Doctrine is the revealed teachings of Scripture regarding the principal beliefs for the Christian faith." According to Martin Manser, "Doctrine is grounded in Scripture and aims to maintain the integrity of Christianity by distinguishing it from non-Christian beliefs. Doctrine is of central importance in Christian preaching and teaching in that it equips the people of God for effective and faithful service in his world."[3]

But how does this relate to biblical theology? Theology is the study of God—*Theo,* meaning "God," and *logy,* meaning "the study of." If we are studying God, are we studying doctrine? Absolutely! However, *doctrine,* as Wayne Grudem defines it, is "what the whole Bible teaches us today about some particular topic."[4] When we as messengers study and teach biblical doctrine, we are addressing a specific teaching in the scope of all biblical theology (the study of God). Dr. James Hamilton defines "doing" biblical theology this way: "To do biblical theology is to think about the whole story of the Bible. We want to understand the organic development of the Bible's

---

3   Martin H. Manser, Alister E. McGrath, J. I. Packer, and Donald J. Wiseman, eds., *Zondervan Dictionary of Bible Themes: An Accessible and Comprehensive Tool for Topical Studies,* Logos Bible Software (Grand Rapids: Zondervan, 1999), sec. #8234.

4   Wayne A. Grudem, *Systematic Theology: An Introduction to Biblical Doctrine* (Grand Rapids: Zondervan, 1994), 25.

teaching so that we are interpreting particular parts of the story in light of the whole."[5]

So to study and teach biblical doctrine is to draw out a specific teaching from the entire scope of our biblical theology. As missionaries, our theology should be constructed on the doctrines of Scripture; therefore, theology is everything believers need for spiritual growth. We cannot have one without the other. When people ask me, "What is your theology?" First, I ask, "Which part?" Because what we study and believe about the doctrines of Scripture will define our theology. When asked about my theology, I usually start with Genesis 3:15: "I will put enmity between you and the woman, and between your offspring and her offspring; he shall bruise your head, and you shall bruise his heel." All our theology as ministers of the gospel springs from this one verse because this is the promise and foretelling of the Lord of all glory, Christ, who will be born from the seed of the woman to destroy the seed of the serpent. This is a supernatural prophecy that proves our doctrine is truthful and worthy of all our labors.

If theology is so vital to our mission, why are some churches and mission organizations commissioning people to preach and teach the gospel without confirming their doctrinal clarity? Why are there missionaries who cannot teach theology? Why do some missionaries find theology insignificant? Where has this crisis come from? What can missionaries, the church, and mission organizations do to combat it? This chapter addresses these questions.

Biblical doctrine is essential. To refuse to teach it to believers is to disobey God's Word: "What you have heard from me [the apostle Paul] in the presence of many witnesses entrust to faithful men, who will be able to teach others also" (2 Tim. 2:2). Four generations are mentioned in this one verse. Teaching biblical doctrine is a command for missionaries so that those we instruct can turn around and educate other faithful

---

5   James M. Hamilton, Jr., *What Is Biblical Theology?: A Guide to the Bible's Story, Symbolism, and Patterns* (Wheaton, IL: Crossway, 2014), 12.

believers. Teaching doctrine is indispensable in missions. We must never think that this command is just for pastors. Missionaries do the work of pastors. In studying and teaching biblical doctrine, we learn about and come to know this massive God who told Ezekiel, "Son of man, feed your belly with this scroll that I give you and fill your stomach with it" (Ezek. 3:3). We learn the beautiful truths of the God who saved us. We learn about his character, heart, mind, desires, will, and commands. And then we pass these beautiful, powerful truths to others. Men and women need biblical doctrine. Without it we wither up and die in our ignorance of the truth and never know the divine glories of the Trinity.

A danger in the American church and in American mission organizations (not all—there are good ones—but many) is to send missionaries who dilute the authority of Scripture. They present biblical doctrines as mere overtones, commissioning men and women who are unequipped, ill-prepared, and too immature to handle the doctrines of our Lord, let alone who believe they are vital for making disciples and for progressive sanctification.

One afternoon, I was riding through the city of Bandung in a taxi van with several other missionaries from around the world. We were invited to the home of one of our language teachers outside the city. As we were talking, one young man turned to me and asked, "Do you believe that God would send people to hell for their sin?" I said, "Yes, I do believe that." I showed him many verses in Scripture that prove that God is "just and the justifier" (Rom. 3:26). I explained that God's wrath upon sinners is fully just, serving his justice to many by casting them into hell, and it shows mercy to many by saving them from their sin and its judgment. Many of the other language students in the van were listening, but they did not comment. The young man went on to say, "I do not think a loving God would send people to hell." The beliefs he had about God are terrible indeed. But this is not the only problem. He had no idea about the nature, character, and attributes of God, and yet he was sent by a mission organization to a Muslim country to "tell" people about Jesus.

In America over the last few years, there has been such a push to send missionaries to foreign fields that we have rushed the process. Half the time we do not fully know what people believe or what they teach others.

We must send missionaries to people groups that have never heard of our Jesus—it is vital. In fact, Scripture teaches us to pray for more laborers because there are few (Luke 10:2), but the danger is that there is so much hype in "going and sending" that the senders often forget to test the goers in their doctrine. In Matthew 28:19–20, Jesus said, "Go therefore and make disciples of all nations, baptizing them in the name of the Father and of the Son and of the Holy Spirit, teaching them to observe all that I have commanded you." This command to "teach them to observe all ... I have commanded you" has become a new trendy fad in which people go to "share" the gospel, get people to say a repeated prayer, and then pack their bags and return to the States with marvelous stories of how God used them to save the lost. Or people move to a foreign country to share the gospel but never once teach the doctrines of Scripture, and then their people are left drowning in a river of confusion that will eventually lead them into heresy. I have seen it on the field, and my heart breaks for those men and women who desire truth but have a missionary who does not teach sound biblical doctrine.

There are two popular reasons for this oversight on the part of the missionary. One is that many missionaries simply do not understand the doctrines of Scripture, so they do not even attempt to teach them. Why? The church has not done its biblical duty to train, instruct, and correct them. It could be that they have not had the proper biblical training from an institution under the guidance of a local church. I will address these problems in more depth later in the chapter.

The second is a belief that the doctrines of Scripture are too heavy for uneducated believers. Like the example I gave in the opening of this chapter, so too are many missionaries embracing this type of approach. We know from Scripture that new believers, whether educated or not, need milk, but as they grow, they need meat (Heb. 5:12). Uneducated believers are just as capable as learning doctrine as educated ones.

Perhaps this trend has surfaced from the model, assist, watch, and leave (MAWL) method. This model, as M. David Sills explains, "often seeks only to train nationals to repeat the church planting experience, not giving them the thorough biblical knowledge and sound doctrinal grounding that they need."[6] The missionaries who hold such views have never slogged through the daily teaching of sound doctrine only to see that these believers need even more the next day. Because the missionaries have never taught it, they do not realize what is missing and how much these new believers need solid doctrinal teaching.

In my ministry to the Korowai in interior Papua, I would preach the truths of Scripture, the beautiful doctrines of the Word of God, day after day and week after week, only to see them turn around the next minute and do the very opposite of what I labored so hard to teach, which is all the more reason they need it every single day. A vivid example occurred one morning when I was teaching on the commands for husbands to love their wives, wives to respect their husbands, and fathers not to provoke their children to anger but bring them up in the discipline of the Lord (Eph. 5:33; 6:4). This was a completely new concept in Korowai culture—they had never heard anything like it. I had been teaching these doctrines for months. On this morning after the lesson, a Korowai man went out the door, picked up his child and held him upside down by the ankles, and began to beat the child on the head with a stick. The only thing the child had done was whine at him. Teaching doctrine day after day with seemingly no results can be extremely disheartening, but it must become a daily habit before it can begin to affect lives.

---

6   M. David Sills, *Reaching and Teaching: A Call to Great Commission Obedience.* (Chicago: Moody, 2010), 49.

Although teaching biblical doctrine is a continuous, difficult job, it has eternal rewards. Doctrine is vital for the continuing sanctifying work of the Holy Spirit in believers' lives. It is essential to our faith. As missionaries, we are helping to prepare Christ's bride, so we must take every effort to make that bride as beautiful for him as possible through patient, thorough edification.

Are We Qualified?

The Great Commission is the highest charge our Creator has given us. I can think of nothing better in this life than to be sent by my King to herald his message to those who do not yet know him and teach believers so that they will in turn grow in spiritual maturity and worship the Lord. This is a high calling and one that we do not deserve. Do you still marvel that God chose you out of so many and sent you to a foreign people to preach and teach the good news? I hope that as missionaries of our Lord Jesus Christ, we constantly bow to him in humility, recognizing that we are not, in our own strength, qualified to serve as we do.

Who is qualified? Was the man who told the Papuan evangelists they did not need doctrine qualified? Anyone who carefully studies Scripture would say no. A person who says such a thing on the mission field should go home. If we are not teaching biblical doctrine to the people we are sent to, we have no business being there. Some people will ask, "What about medical missionaries or missionary pilots?" This question should not call for a different answer. Even these types of missionaries must study and know sound biblical doctrine. No missionary has any excuse, no matter what job he or she is doing. All missionaries must consider themselves equal to the task of knowing biblical doctrine.

What does it take to be a missionary who teaches sound biblical doctrine? Paul writes to Titus concerning elders: "He must hold firm to the trustworthy word as taught, so that he may be able to give instruction in sound doctrine and also to rebuke those who contradict it" (Titus 1:9). I am not going to give a lengthy exposition on this verse, but I want you to notice several words Paul uses.

First, notice the phrase "hold firm." These two words form the Greek verb *antechomenon*, which means "to be devoted; to give oneself entirely to a specific activity, person, or cause."[7] This is a middle or passive accusative verb. That means that the subject, being a man, is not only the agent of the action but is doing the action for his own interests. This makes sense because Paul uses a *hina* clause in the latter part of the verse to show the outcome of a person's action and concern for his own interests in the action. Paul is telling Titus that a man must be solely devoted, giving himself fully to doctrine and keep that doctrine for himself. Why? He gives two reasons to be devoted to biblical doctrine: "so that he may be able to give instruction in sound doctrine and also to rebuke those who contradict it." Throughout this text, the stated goal is to exhort believers in sound doctrine and to warn and silence unbelievers.

Notice the phrase "be able to." This is the Greek phrase *eimi kai dynatos*, which means "having the necessary means, skill, know-how, or authority (to do something)."[8] A man must be skillful and competent in the divine duties of doctrinal instruction. He must learn these things and put them into practice, not only for the people he will teach but also for himself. Paul is describing what an elder of the church must have to hold this high heavenly position. It is the same thing the missionary must commit to for a life of service.

We do not just herald the salvation story and then focus solely on translation or humanitarian action. No, we move from proclaiming the gospel to proclaiming the gospel, again and again and again. In that repetitive laboring, we teach the doctrines of Scripture. Missionaries can focus on their translation and health efforts while teaching biblical doctrine. We

---

7   *The Bible Sense Lexicon*, s.v. "*antechomenon*," https://ref.ly/logos4/Senses?KeyId=ws.be+devoted.v.01.

8   *The Bible Sense Lexicon*, s.v. "*Eimi kai dynatos*," https://ref.ly/logos4/Senses?KeyId=ws.able.a.01.

should never place other endeavors above teaching biblical doctrine. Missionaries must teach at least the following:

1. The doctrine of God the Father,
2. the doctrine of Jesus Christ,
3. the doctrine of the Holy Spirit,
4. the doctrine of the Scriptures
5. the doctrine of man,
6. the doctrine of salvation,
7. the doctrine of the church,
8. the doctrine of prayer, and
9. the doctrine of glorification.

Within these doctrines are categories of other doctrines to teach. For example, in the doctrine of man, we would teach who man is and what sin is; but we would also instruct men to love their wives, women to respect their husbands, and fathers to raise their children in godly discipline. Teaching doctrine takes work and time, but the end results are for the glory of the Bridegroom. As missionaries, do we hold firm to the doctrines of Scripture? Do we love them so much that we would be willing to give up our desires to teach them? Even give our lives for them?

I believe that every man sent to preach and teach in a foreign land must meet the qualifications of an elder. Let's look at the requirements for eldership from 1 Timothy 3:1–7:

> The saying is trustworthy: If anyone aspires to the office of overseer, he desires a noble task. Therefore an overseer must be above reproach, the husband of one wife, sober-minded, self-controlled, respectable, hospitable, able to teach, not a drunkard, not violent but gentle, not quarrelsome, not a lover of money. He must manage his own household well, with all dignity keeping his children submissive, for if someone does not know how to manage his own household, how will he care for God's church? He

must not be a recent convert, or he may become puffed up with conceit and fall into the condemnation of the devil. Moreover, he must be well thought of by outsiders, so that he may not fall into disgrace, into a snare of the devil.

Clearly, the desire to be an elder is a high calling and not one to be taken lightly. An elder is called to lead God's people. He shepherds them to worship in spirit and truth (John 4:23). He teaches them sound biblical doctrine (Titus 2:1). He cares for them as his own children (Acts 20:28). Does a missionary do these things on the field? Absolutely! A missionary performs the same work as a pastor in a local church shepherding his congregation. Thus, the desire to be a missionary is also a high calling.

My local church commissioned and ordained me. Although I am not installed as an elder, the church leadership confirmed that I meet the qualifications to be an elder and therefore a missionary. My elders tested and confirmed my doctrine because they did not want to send someone who was unqualified. They also confirmed and tested me because I am an extension of them. As missionaries, we are an extension of our local church. Think about it this way: as missionaries, we are the arm, and our local sending church is the body. It is not merely us on the field, but our local sending church is also there through us. They send us to do the same work as the elders do but in a cross-cultural setting. That is one reason I believe a missionary must be elder qualified.

I believe many churches and missionaries are in danger of thinking too individualistically when it pertains to being an elder and a missionary. They somehow view the two as different institutions. A missionary is being sent to cross ethnolinguistic boundaries, but this does not mean that he is somehow given a free pass regarding elder qualifications. If a person is a missionary, call him such, but truthfully, he must be elder material—he must be elder qualified. When we call an electrician to install electricity or fix a problem, we do not hope that they are capable of doing the job, we trust that they were trained in all points of electrical management to complete the job. It is the same with missionaries. We should not go without being trained, tested, and confirmed in all points of doctrine and meeting the qualifications of eldership. Otherwise, we will not be able to complete the job. It is vital to know doctrine because we not only represent our Lord in preparing his bride, but we also represent our sending church. Paul told Timothy, "being trained in the words of the faith and of the good doctrine that you have followed" (1 Tim. 4:6).

Are you trained in all points of doctrine? Have you been tested and confirmed in your giftings of handling the Word of God? Are you able to teach the doctrines of Scripture with clarity? If not, your responsibility is to make that happen before being sent. Do not think about boarding that plane to be Christ's representative in a foreign field if you do not have your doctrine in order. We do not send soldiers into battle to face the enemy without first putting them through extensive training.

My family and I had been in Danowage for six months. We were out of food and needed rest in the coastal town, so we ordered the plane and flew out to resupply. Because we would be there on Sunday, we decided to attend the expat church in town and looked forward to receiving solid biblical teaching. That morning, another missionary, who had been serving for several years, stood up to preach. He began with a few stories that made the audience laugh. When he finally opened the text and read a portion of Scripture, he said, "I do not know Greek, and I do not know how to do word studies, but..." My heart sinking, I looked at my wife. She knew I was ready to walk out, angry at what could have been an opportunity for solid biblical doctrine for the other missionaries there, including us.

A crisis is taking place in the missionary movement: missionaries do not see the importance of knowing how to handle and teach the Scriptures. Not all missionaries are like this. I know veteran missionaries and new ones alike that put me to shame at how they know and teach the Word of God. I desire to be more like them. But there are also missionaries being sent who cannot teach the biblical doctrines simply because they have never had the proper training and do not study on their own. To be a missionary is to have a life of study. Do you realize that? To be a missionary is to constantly swim in the unreachable depths of the Word. Studying does not end when you reach the mission field. In fact, your dependence on the Lord drives you to study even more so that the people you are ministering to can see the man of God, so they can see Christ shining through you.

I am not writing this book to give you ten steps to achieve biblical and doctrinal clarity. I am writing this book to missionaries, churches, and mission organizations to encourage them to see that missionaries must be trained, tested, and confirmed, that they must study the Scriptures and know their doctrine. May it never be heard from a missionary's lips that he does not know how to study the Bible or that doctrine is not important.

Many churches today are ignorant of how to train a potential missionary. It is not on their radar. I believe this results from a church-driven culture that says the mission organization is responsible for the missionary. It usually works this way: Potential missionaries approach the church leadership about their call to go overseas. Then they share about a mission organization they would like to go with. The church helps them with the cost of going to the mission organization for candidate school. Or a missionary has already joined a mission organization and needs a sending church. That church sees the missionary already confirmed and accepted by a mission organization and agrees to help send him without fully confirming his gifts. Church fellowships and associations, including several mission organizations, are beginning to recognize this mistake. Nevertheless, it is a crisis that will only grow if we do not change what we are doing.

Some churches and mission organizations have forgotten or do not realize that to send missionaries to people who do

not know Christ is to place them on the front lines of battle.
We face a clever enemy. Why would we send a missionary
into battle without the proper armor? When a missionary is in
the thick of ministry, a battle rages on the mission field. I have
been there. The stresses of a third-world culture life; incessant
heat that drains you; rashes, boils, infections, malaria, dengue,
and chikungunya that plague the body;[9] never-ending noise of
people sitting at your door and the constant begging for things;
violent men that storm around your house, men threatening
you with bows and arrows and swinging machetes at you and
people throwing rocks at you; your sick child you worry about
and cannot get a flight out of the jungle for; relentless mildew-
ing of your possessions and the perpetual repairs necessary to
continue living there; being wet for days on end because of the
weather; the incessant scratching of pigs that keep you awake
at night by rubbing themselves on your foundation poles; fights
that break out in the village; the lack of food in the house from
low supplies, your co-workers not being there and you needing
to handle everything on your own; continual government visits
that take your time; 24/7 healthcare work and sick people who
need your attention three times a day; the deaths of people
you have been treating and children who perish because of
evil fathers; the constant needs of your evangelist team and
deaths of your evangelist team members; frequent requests
for medevacs, unremitting domestic abuses in the village, and
worry and care for young girls who are forced into marriage;
hiking through knee-deep mud, recurring boat rides to different
villages, and daily translation of their language; time needed
with your wife and children and family worship; and then, the

---

9 *Chikungunya* is a tropical arboviral infection transmitted by mosquitoes. It
causes fever, chills, headache, muscle pains, severe joint pains, eye pain, rash,
sore throat, and vomiting. There is no cure for this illness, only supportive care.
Joint pains can persist for years after contact. *Dengue* is a tropical arboviral fever
transmitted by mosquitoes. It causes high fever, severe body pains, eye pain,
headaches, rash, insomnia, nightmares, depression, and hallucinations. There
is no cure for dengue, only supportive care. Symptoms generally last for two
weeks, although depression and fatigue can persist for years after contact. See
Mary Vanderkooi, *The Village Medical Manual: A Layman's Guide to Health Care
in Developing Countries*, 6th ed. (Pasadena, CA: William Carey Library, 2009),
187, 197–199.

daily preaching of the gospel and teaching of biblical doctrine. Why would the church send a missionary to this kind of life without first equipping him in all points of biblical doctrine?

And why would we send a missionary to this kind of life without first checking his/her personal life? I pray I never hear a church say they just do not have time in their schedule to train men for the ministry. Once a man enters this kind of ministry, the battle for time alone with God begins. My wife and I finally came up with a plan. I would hide myself in my hot, stuffy office area until 11:00 a.m. If anything came up in the village, I was not available until noon, after I had eaten lunch with my family, unless it was an emergency. After noon, I was all theirs. The study of Scripture is so important that we must, as ministers of the gospel, hide, if necessary, to commune with our Lord. And it will benefit the people as well.

Dear Church

Doctrine and study go together. Your missionaries will not learn and grow in biblical doctrine unless they study. Church leaders, do you see a passion to study in your missionaries? This is a priority. Missionaries must have a solid foundation through their local sending church to reach the mission field.

When I was converted, I joined a church, and the pastor invested in me. He discipled, groomed, and mentored me. He prepared me for the labors of preaching the gospel in a foreign field. We met several times a week, and he discipled me over and over. He not only taught me biblical doctrine but also worked through the jungle of messes I had made in my unsaved state. This continued for four years.

About a year and a half after he started discipling me, he asked, "Would you like to teach at the nursing home this Saturday night?"

My stomach churned. "Yes!" I blurted out. I could not believe what I had just said. "How long should I teach?"

"Fifteen to twenty minutes," he responded.

I nervously worked all week to prepare for twenty minutes of teaching. I spoke from Philippians 1 on joy, and I still remember that blessed time. My pastor listened to me teach, and then we reviewed the sermon together. Through godly counsel and instruction he helped me further sharpen my preaching. If it weren't for this dear man, I would not be where I am today. He taught me doctrine and gave me ample opportunity to refine and use my giftings each week in the church. I exercised my spiritual gifts that would later be applied in a remote jungle tribe. Because of this pastor's discipleship and mentorship, I was able to use the same principles he instilled in me as I discipled the Lani evangelists and the Korowai believers we serve with in Papua.

Church leaders, what are you doing to prepare your missionaries for lives of service? As church leaders, are you intentionally seeking out those within your congregation to disciple, groom, mentor, and teach? Are you giving them opportunities to sharpen and use their spiritual gifts? Are you investing in their lives and helping them work through the tough baggage they may still carry from their former sinful lives?

I firmly believe that the church should change its thinking about how missionaries prepare for the field. No longer should it merely be the missionaries approaching the leadership about pursuing missions or finding their own biblical training, but church leaders must be active in approaching men and woman within the church body about serving long-term overseas. If churches are training and discipling men and women and allowing them to use their spiritual gifts, they will clearly see whether they are qualified to do the work of missionaries. If churches did this, we would not hear men telling national Christians that doctrine is unimportant. The reminder in 2 Timothy 2:2 that says, "what you have heard from me in the presence of many witnesses entrust to faithful men, who will be able to teach others also," must be the fuel that fires the all-consuming, never-ending work to send qualified and equipped missionaries. Church leaders, you can be involved in countless generations of men who learn and teach biblical doctrine. Remember, 2 Timothy 2:2 is a command, not an option.

If the local church is the sending church, then it must not bow to modern trends such as allowing the missionary alone to choose the organization, have the mission organization be the missionary's sole sender, depend on the mission organization to equip the missionary, depend on the seminary to equip the missionary, or depend on the missionary's personal biblical studies. I know of several mission organizations and seminaries that cooperate with local churches in preparing potential missionaries. They are doing great work in coming alongside the local church. I believe that is biblical. But if the church places all the responsibility on some other person, organization, or school, then the church is not modeling the New Testament mandate.

When I moved from North Carolina to Minnesota, my sending church in Minnesota would not send me out as a missionary until I was equipped. The leadership allowed me to serve for two years while being trained, discipled, mentored, and groomed (that did not include the four years in North Carolina). I am thankful for leadership who did not leave me on my own. They were intentional and engaging in my preparation. I would not be where I am today if the local church had just thrown me over to an organization to fend for myself. Many missionaries on the field are in dire need of training and struggle in multiple areas of their ministry simply because they lack an engaging sending church in their preparation and while on the field. We must do an overhaul in our efforts to send missionaries who are equipped and trained in biblical doctrine.

What about women? How can they be qualified? This is a serious query that needs gentle yet clear explanation from Scripture. Here is my conviction to churches concerning women being sent in full-time missionary work.

First, theology is not just for men. A huge misunderstanding in the church is to teach the men theology and do other activities for the women. This is wrong. Theology is for women also.

They must know doctrine backward and forward through their fathers, husbands, and the local church's teaching.

Let me be upfront and honest without delving too far into women's roles in the church. The Scriptures are clear that women are not to teach or exercise authority over men (1 Tim. 2:12). Therefore, I believe that a missionary woman must meet the qualifications of a deacon. Why? The word *servant* (Greek *diakonos*) in 1 Timothy 3:8, 12 means "waiter or servant." This word is associated with several women, such as Martha when she was busy serving the Lord at his table (Luke 10:40); Peter's mother-in-law when Jesus healed her and she began to serve him (Mark 1:31); and "Phoebe, a servant of the church at Cenchreae" (Rom. 16:1). Paul uses this same word for *deacon* in 1 Timothy 3:8. Even though Paul does not use the feminine form, Sinton writes, "The Greek Fathers regularly read 1 Timothy 3:11, 'The women likewise must be serious,' as a reference to the qualities required for women deacons rather than deacon's wives."[10] The bottom line is whether there were deaconesses in the first century or not; we know by these few verses that women served the church and aided the apostles' ministry.

Women serving as missionaries must also meet the qualifications of deacons because every indication in the New Testament, when referring to women, only shows the possibility as a deacon-type ministry. Therefore, I believe missionary women are to be deacon qualified and know their biblical doctrine so they can teach the women and children in their people group, whether single or married. This does not mean that every woman has the gift of teaching. I know many missionary women who have other giftings, and that is a good thing. However, if a church sends a woman to the mission field, she must be trained and tested.

The church must do a better job with its missionary efforts to the nations. As a missionary, I am pleased with what I am seeing in several churches regarding training men and women

---

10   New Bible Dictionary, s.v., "deaconess" (V.M. Sinton), 262.

for long-term missionary work. However, from what is happening on the field now, we have a long way to go. Church leaders, please give yourselves to your missionaries. The eternal rewards are priceless. There are many believers drowning in bad theology because of missionaries that have not been adequately trained. Train, groom, mentor, and prepare them so they will bear much fruit for our Lord Jesus Christ.

Dear Mission Organization

The question we must ask regarding mission organizations is, What can you do to cause a tidal wave of goers who are doctrinally prepared? The answer is simple: Never consider potential missionaries if they are not trained, tested, and confirmed by their local church.

I am not referring to you listening to the potential missionary give a five-minute gospel presentation, but to extensive doctrinal training to ensure the missionary can teach theological points concerning essential and nonessential doctrines. Any church leadership worth their salt will not partner with a mission organization unless they see their candidate already meets the qualifications of an elder or deacon. However, if your organization is equipped for extensive theological training and that training is done in agreement with the local church, then train that missionary.

I know of several organizations that accept candidates without going through their local church or testing their doctrine. They do not check with the local church leadership about the candidate. Mission organizations must be proactive in coming alongside the church with the attitude of, "What can we do to help you as a church send this person with doctrinal clarity to the people group you desire?" If mission organizations had this attitude, we would see fewer missionaries fumbling around in error and silence on the field and find more qualified and hardy people working there instead.

Many mission organizations have not prioritized doctrinal clarity and its importance in the missionary's life and in gospel efforts. They are so worried about being a "mom and pop shop" (a little, no-named mission organization) that they prioritize recruiting over quality. Recruiting is huge among colleges, seminaries, and conferences. A recruiter should ask a potential missionary "Who is your sending church, and are they training you in the doctrines of Scripture?" Let it never be said that you set numbers (missionaries sent, for example) over biblical doctrine.

When I was ten, my parents informed my sister and me that we were moving to Australia as missionaries. Although we were told it would take several years to raise support and prepare for living there, my dear father, bless his heart, raised what we needed in twenty-one months. He worked hard to provide for us and acquire enough money to move his family to a new culture. Yet, what I did not know as a young boy was that never once did his local church and mission organization work together, communicate, or examine his doctrine to see if he was qualified to be sent. His mission organization asked a few surface-level doctrinal questions during his candidate schooling, but they never checked with or assisted his sending church to verify his doctrine and qualifications through the local elders. This was the norm for most churches and mission organizations in the '80s and '90s. Praise the Lord my father was qualified and able to do the work of a pastor/evangelist overseas even though he was not truly confirmed (examined and tested) through his church and mission organization.

Mission organizations, you should not step within a hundred feet of a potential missionary without first checking with his local church leadership and their commitment to doctrinal clarity and service within that local body. If mission organizations committed to checking biblical doctrine first within the life of the candidate through the local church, this would solve much confusion and mitigate potential disaster on the field.

While my father was on the field, there was no real ongoing involvement, accountability, or continual discipleship by his sending church or mission organization. When I contemplate what my parents faced on the field, I am disappointed that they missed out on what could have been a sweet relationship replete with all the benefits, biblically speaking, between the church and the mission organization.

Mission organizations should be in harmony with the local church regarding the missionary's doctrinal life, even after they are on the field. Missionary work is a dangerous calling. What I mean is that mission organizations sometimes forget that missionaries need theology daily to survive on the field. If the missionary's local church is not providing what he/she needs on the field, this is the opportunity to come alongside the local church to encourage the missionary in further doctrinal study. Offer training to a local church to equip its leaders to see the responsibility God has given them as senders of messengers to a foreign field. We must not believe the lie that missionaries are prepared to live on the field if they can give a five- or ten-minute gospel presentation. This is dangerous. If mission organizations make doctrinal clarity and the testing of potential missionaries' doctrine a priority through the local church, we will see much fruit borne for the Lord Jesus Christ, and it will cause other missionaries to realize what they too can have through cooperation and partnership with their local church and mission organization.

I have seen it all too often—potential missionaries are so eager to get to the field that they sometimes do not think clearly. I applaud their zeal, but the candidate needs a mission organization that is mature and patient enough to say, "We need to check your doctrine and qualifications through your local church, and if they agree and you meet all of the criteria, we will talk further."

Father in heaven, I beg you to send more laborers to the harvest. There are only a few. For the glory of your name, would you prepare men and women with doctrinal clarity and understanding, who are able to lead with all honor and purity in the gospel and possess the boldness to proclaim and teach the Scriptures? Would you cause missionaries to recognize the significance of doctrine in their own lives and in the lives of those they serve?

Would you give local churches the ability and wisdom to see the importance of training men and women for this high calling and convict church leaders to give themselves wholly to this effort? Would you please give mission organizations a biblical under- standing of their role in working with the local church? Help them to seek the doctrines of Scripture above all else because in them we see the very heart of Christ and his teachings.

Help the missionary, the local church, and the mission organiza- tion to be as one in fulfilling your command to send out labor- ers. Oh Lord, help us come back to the reality of working side by side with total doctrinal clarity so that this crisis will be snuffed out by sound, biblically qualified men and women. Amen.

3

A Missionary's Prayer Life

One of my favorite nineteenth-century missionaries is John Paton. Never have I read a biography that gripped my heart the way his does. What makes him special in the world of foreign missions is something that he observed as a child and remembered until his death: John had a special father. Mr. Paton was a man of prayer, and his influence helped shape his son to become the man we know as the Missionary to the New Hebrides.

In his biography, John wrote this of his father:

> Thither daily, and often times a day, generally after each meal, we saw our father retire, and 'shut to the door'; and we children got to understand by sort of spiritual instinct (for the thing was too sacred to be talked about) that prayers were being poured out there for us, as of old by the High Priest within the veil in the Most Holy Place. We occasionally heard the pathetic echoes of a trembling voice pleading as if for life, and we learned to slip out and in past that door on tiptoe, not to disturb the holy colloquy.

> The outside world might not know, but we knew, whence came that happy light as of a new-born smile that always was dawning on my father's face: it was a reflection from the Divine Presence, in the consciousness of which he lived. . . . My soul would wander back to those early scenes, and shut itself up once again in that Sanctuary Closet, and, hearing still the echoes of those cries to God, would hurl back all doubt with victorious appeal, 'He walked with God, why may not I.'[1]

This phrase particularly convicted me: "it was a reflection from the Divine Presence, in the consciousness of which he lived." When I read that, I was deeply moved in my soul. Do I consciously live like that before God and my family? Is my prayer life consumed with meeting his divine presence as if my life depended on it? Does my countenance prove I am lost in the pleadings of prayer to my God?

Initially, I was nervous about including this chapter because as I reflect on my years as a missionary, I see the countless opportunities where I could have been more faithful in prayer with God. Think about how much sweet, divine communion we pass up in the daily grind of tough ministry because we deem what we are doing as imperative. Rather, we should be hoarding all the communion with our God that we can in order to appreciate him and become more like him and receive the blessings and rewards in our lives and ministries that will follow consistent communion with his holiness. No missionary, or believer for that matter, can "do" ministry without prayer. We are dependent on God and God alone.

As I pondered the missionary life and what I could write about prayer, I was reminded of Matthew 6:6: "But when you pray, go into your room and shut the door and pray to your Father who is in secret. And your Father who sees in secret will reward you." Why this verse? John Paton's father threw

---

1   John G. Paton, *John G. Paton: Missionary to the New Hebrides, An Autobiography*, edited by James Paton (Carlisle, PA: Banner of Truth, 1965), 8.

away the cares of the world to spend time in prayer with his Sovereign. He did this in private, alone, and for the sake of his soul and his family's souls. He gave up time with his family and friends as well as other important matters to be alone with God. He counted the time with his Lord more important than anything because he knew the everlasting results of that divine communion. Prayer to the Almighty has eternal, sanctifying, intimate, and rewarding results. John's father knew this. To lose that abiding communion with the King would bring damaging consequences to his soul.

Of all the verses on prayer, why is Matthew 6:6 so important? If any missionary knows the struggles of being alone with God, I do. No missionary would admit to praying too often or spending too much time alone with God. They cannot because they do not. If you ever hear a missionary say those words, beware; it is not the truth. What then can we glean from this text in Matthew concerning prayer?

The context of this passage informs us that Jesus is instructing the Jews to pray with the right heart attitude. Self-righteous, self-centered, self-aggrandizing, long, wordy, and phony prayers are the sins Jesus addresses in these verses. Notice his words at the beginning of verse 5: "And when you pray." It was not a question of "if" we pray but "when." Prayer is essential for believers. John MacArthur says, "Prayer is the constant inhale, exhale of communion with God that goes on in the life of a believer all the time. Not to pray is to hold your breath."[2] To pray is to breathe. When we commune with our God in prayer, we live. In prayer, we live in sweet, divine communion with him. When we do not pray, we are holding our breath and suffocating under intense discomfort and pain, always on the verge of passing out from lack of oxygen, and eventually we die. That is how serious prayer is for believers. Jesus told his disciples, "Stay awake at all times, praying that you may have strength to escape all these things that are going to take place"

---

2   John MacArthur, "Praying Without Hypocrisy," Grace to You, October 21, 1979, https://www.gty.org/library/sermons-library/2230/praying-without-hypo crisy.

(Luke 21:36). I am writing on this subject because if you are like this missionary (me), you need to "stay awake" and be alone with your Lord in his sanctuary.

Prayer on the Mission Field

When it comes to prayer, missionaries do not possess more power, discipline, or will than other believers. We have been granted access to the throne of God for communion and worship. Before him, we are the same. In our daily lives, we are dependent on God for our progressive sanctification. In foreign missions, missionaries rely on God for their own sanctification but also for the salvation of the souls they are ministering to.

I know the tendency of the missionary life all too well. Missionaries can forget that their ministries are dependent on God's favor and his work through the power of his Spirit. Life gets busy and forgetfulness sets in easily. Jungle life is difficult. If you have a ministry like mine, you are never alone. People are always at your house, which is mostly screen so we do not smother from the heat and which means we hear everything. Being alone takes on a different definition in this kind of ministry. The Korowai are an individualistic culture, but in recent years, they have moved from their tree houses as single-family units to multiple families living in one village. Many clans live together, and those clans are constantly at our door. For missionaries to enter this kind of culture is to say goodbye to the Western mindset of individualism and, in part, to being alone.

If the missionary life is that difficult, how can we be alone with God? Is being alone with God essential for both the missionary and the ministry? How can missionaries "pray without ceasing" (1 Thess. 5:17) when given such ministries? Are missionaries to surrender certain rights, such as being alone with God, for the people we serve? Are those people more important than being alone with God?

In this section, I want to unpack these questions for a deeper understanding of what a missionary's prayer life should look like. Charles Haddon Spurgeon has an excellent thought concerning prayer: "A Christian should carry the weapon of all prayer like a drawn sword in his hand."[3] Prayer should be our first, automatic response. Prayer will only become an automatic response in our lives and ministry when we devote ourselves to rigorous deep communion with God. I genuinely believe that if a missionary is not committed to being alone with God every day in prayer with thanksgivings and pleadings, then the recurring discipline that we must have of praying throughout the day's activities will be nonexistent and void of his power. It is crucial that we have communion with God alone, which will lead to a lifestyle of prayer in our daily ministry.

One Sunday morning in Danowage, I woke up early to look over my Scriptures and notes for preaching God's Word to the Korowai. After my family and I had breakfast, we headed out to trample through the mud toward the church building. As we started the walk, I heard loud shouting and commotion where the paths crossed near the Korowai huts. As we got closer, the hollering became screaming, and the village people were running toward the sound to see what was going on. When my family and I reached the village center, I told my wife and children to stay there while I went to assess the situation. By this time, the whole village had assembled, and I knew that worship would be on hold for a while. I walked farther down and saw the village chief, Tomas, and another Korowai man named Peter yelling at one another. From the sound of it, they were fighting over a woman in another village.

Peter, bow and arrows drawn, stormed around Tomas's house, demanding that he come out and pay for what he had done. Threats flew back and forth. Tomas screamed at Peter from inside his hut. Peter kept his bow drawn, stomping around, occasionally hitting Tomas's house in anger. As I watched this unfold, I could feel the eyes of the entire village resting on me. What would I do? What would I say?

---

3   Charles Spurgeon, quoted in John MacArthur, *Alone with God: Rediscovering the Power and Passion of Prayer* (Colorado Springs: David C. Cook, 2011), 18.

I could feel the anger boiling in my stomach, especially because it was Sunday morning, and we were preparing for worship. I was twenty feet from Tomas's house watching this, and then I glanced over at a small, round-shaped tree beside the path not far from where I stood. Everyone could see this tree. I gazed at it as the men continued their fight, and privately I asked God if he would please strike that tree with his power like he did with Moses and the burning bush so that the entire Korowai village would see his glory and, in turn, fall to their knees in fear and repent, especially Tomas and Peter. After all, what could I do? I am just a man. God could strike that tree with lightning and jolt everyone to listen and live in peace if he wanted to, right? But I knew that God does not typically work in those ways, even though I prayed for it and wished it would happen.

"Lord, what will it take to get their attention?" I prayed in my heart. "Please do something. This is your day so we can worship you." As soon as I prayed, "Lord, show them their sin. Do something!" a flood came over me, and I shouted at the top of my lungs, "What are you doing? Every day I live here with you, teaching you the Word of God and living here to help you. Why is it that every Sunday morning you want to fight? God sees what you are doing, and he is angry with you. Maybe I should go to another people and live with them. Maybe they will listen to me. God is angry with your behavior. Look, the women and children are watching you act like this. You need to stop and repent of your sin. I want to go worship, and you are acting like Satan. I am going to the church building, and you will stop this right now."

I had never raised my voice like that before. You could have heard a pin drop. No one spoke. It was as if the Lord had given me righteous anger in answer to my desperate prayer. It felt like I was not the one speaking. Without waiting for a response, I turned around and headed to the church, still feeling worked up. Slowly, most everyone made their way to the building. When I stood up to preach that morning, I saw Peter sitting there, listening intently to what I was saying. From that time on, I never had another problem with Peter. Tomas is another book of stories I could write. He did not come that morning, nor has he yet changed in his character. I still pray for him.

What is the point of this story? There is a time and place for such prayers. We should do as Spurgeon says and "carry the weapon of prayer like a drawn sword." Prayer is vital in all situations because it shows that we are weak humans who are dependent on Christ alone.

Almost no missionary has a problem praying in public. In corporate worship, prayer is expected and thought about as second nature. It is part of the job. Hopefully, we were trained before reaching the field that prayer is essential in corporate worship. We know this from the Word of God. Therefore, it is easy to carry the weapon of prayer into a worship setting or a tree house full of tribal people. We should not have to think twice about it. We pray, teach, and pray some more, and that is a good thing. We need to be in a continual mindset of prayer with our Bible teaching and in public worship. After all, are we not as ministers of the gospel to "devote ourselves to prayer and to the ministry of the word" (Acts 6:4)? Of course.

Alone with God on the Mission Field

When it comes to our private life, a shift occurs. Imagine being home with your spouse all day and never saying a word to them. You love this person and would die for them, your best friend. You made a covenant till death do you part. You share the same home and the same room and the same bed. Why would you go all day without speaking? How would your wife or husband feel if you treated them this way? It would not make for a healthy relationship; in fact, there would not be one. And yet this is exactly what many missionaries do to our Lord.

We slog deep in the duties of ministry, exhausting ourselves to help people know the truths of Scripture and understand the gospel, care for the sick, meet people's needs, spend hours talking to people, and yet we come back to our home and never speak to our King. I have been there. I have spent all my energy for the sake of the Korowai to the point of collapse. But private prayer was too hard to do, too much of a task, because after all, people were waiting for me, and I had to make them see how happy I was to help them. Right? This kind of thinking is wrong. Why do we missionaries labor so hard in the ministry and yet forsake fellowship with our King who desires our attention and worship?

To be clear, God does not need anything from us. He is complete in himself. But because of Jesus Christ, we now have intimate fellowship with the Father, and that cherished communion is sustained and grown through prayer. Prayer is our most eminent necessity. Being alone with God is our greatest need. Our greatest need is not to satisfy the people we serve or preach the gospel or treat every sick person. Those things are good and necessary, but not our greatest need. We missionaries need to be alone with God, on our knees lost in his divine presence. Nothing is greater. He has promised blessings and rewards for those who seek him in prayer (Matt. 6:6). We should long for those rewards.

Look at Matthew 6:6 again: "But when you pray, go into your room and shut the door." Notice Jesus did not say, "Go anywhere you want and pray to your Father." We know that praying can be done in any location and at any time. People prayed on the street corner (Matt. 6:5); Jesus prayed in the wilderness (Mark 1:35) and on the cross (Luke 23:34); Peter prayed on the rooftop (Acts 10:9); Paul and Silas went "to the place of prayer" (Acts 16:16); and Paul and Silas prayed in prison (Acts 16:25). We can pray anywhere. However, in Matthew 6, Jesus is teaching his hearers the importance of being alone with God with the right heart attitude. J. C. Ryle states it well:

> It is not enough to join in the prayers of the congregation on Sundays or attend the prayer of a family on week-days. There must be private prayer also. Without this we may be outward members of Christ's church, but we are not living members of

Christ. . . . In praying, the principal object to be sought, is to be alone with God. We should endeavor to find some place where no mortal eye sees us, and where we can pour out our hearts with the feeling that no one is looking at us but God.[4]

Being alone with God means "go into your room and shut the door" (v. 6). The words "go into" are the Greek words *eiselthe eis*, which mean "enter." This is an aorist, active, imperative verb, which means it is a continuous command because there is no time element. The meaning of aorist verbs can be broad, but I believe Jesus is commanding his listeners to enter their own place of solitude with urgency and solemnity. Doing so is to be a top priority. This is not a suggestion but a command. The word *room* is the Greek word *tameion*, referring to one's inner room. Literally, it means a storage room where one would keep his possessions.[5] This room is in the inner parts of the house where no one would bother him.

Jesus highlights the importance of this duty even further by saying "shut the door." Prevent any opening, lock the door, bar it so no one can see you and no one can get in. This is to be a sanctuary for meeting the divine presence, the Holy One. No one needs to see us. No one should interrupt what is taking place behind these closed doors. It is too sweet and beautiful to put on display. This act of worship is private between God and man alone.

Do you see the significance of this command? That God the Father would summon us to his sanctuary alone is the highest calling. Even earthly kings do not invite many of their subjects, yet the King of the universe bids us to come and dine with him alone in intimate prayer, to attend a one-on-one meeting done in secret. Who would refuse to meet secretly with an earthly king? Why then would we refuse to meet with our heavenly King? To refuse is to lose rewards, to insult the King,

---

4   J. C. Ryle, *Ryle's Expository Thoughts on the Gospels, Vol. 1: Matthew–Mark* (Grand Rapids: Baker Book House, 1977), 47–48.

5   *The Bible Sense Lexicon*, s.v. "*tameion*," https://ref.ly/logos4/Senses?KeyId=ws.inner+room.n.01.

to dishonor him. The only way we will live and survive on the mission field is when we consistently meet with God alone in our room with the door barred.

Missionaries often appear spiritually healthy. They act sober in communion, inspire and lead others in godly duties, and have many ministry stories to tell. But when alone, they do not seek to speak with their master. The truth is that no one sees our prayer life. The only time other believers glimpse a missionary's prayer life is when he stands up to preach or prays publicly. The only people who will ever truly know someone's personal prayer life are his spouse and children. Our families will see how often we are alone with God. Do our eyes gaze past the people we love, not because we lack love for them or want to avoid them, but because we desire more than anything to speak with our Lord? You and your family are the only people who know if you are obeying Christ's command to enter your room and pray in secret.

We must be alone with God for at least two important reasons, and these two come from personal experience and conviction and are the ones I need to highlight here. If I could redo some of those years in Papua with a greater passion and sense of the need to "go into your room and shut the door," I would gladly lock arms with my Lord even more in private prayer. I do not want missionaries to learn the need and importance of prayer through neglect.

The Battle for Holiness

The first reason to be alone with God is to win the battle for holiness. Colossians 4:2 says, "Continue steadfastly in prayer, being watchful in it with thanksgiving," and Jesus tells his disciples, "Watch and pray that you may not enter into temptation" (Matt. 26:41). These two verses have something in common: the command to watch. Why do the Scriptures place so much emphasis on "watching" in prayer?

In these two verses, the word *watch* is the Greek word *gregoreo*, which means "to be alert, to stay awake, to beware, to be in constant readiness."[6] In both instances, it is a present active verb. This is not an "alertness" that manifests during some future trouble but a daily ongoing alertness that never sleeps. Alertness and prayer go hand in hand. When we are alert and in a state of readiness concerning our fight for holiness and against the temptation that would rob us of it, as well as our need for Christ's Spirit to fight for us in our most desperate hours, we can enter that secret dwelling room of prayer to seek his strength. This fight for holiness will exhaust the heart, mind, will, emotions, and our strength because we are sinful and have no hope of overcoming our flesh and its desires if we do not stay awake in prayer and depend on Christ for victory. We must expend our energy and battle in our inner room for the sake of holiness.

Because we have been given the huge responsibility of preparing Christ's bride does not mean we are immune to sin. Of all people, we must grow in our holiness because we need his grace as his servants of the gospel. When we enter our inner room, we have an intimate knowledge and fellowship with the Father, and we can seek victory over sin and our flesh when we commune in private with him. Jesus told Peter, James, and John, "Watch and pray that you may not enter into temptation" (Matt. 26:41). The temptation to sin will still happen. Jesus also told his disciples, "Temptations to sin are sure to come, but woe to the one through whom they come!" (Luke 17:1). We will be tempted to sin until the day we die. Therefore, this is more reason we must be on high alert every minute.

Paul warned the Ephesians to pray "at all times in the Spirit, with all prayer and supplication. To that end keep alert with all perseverance, making supplication for all the saints" (Eph. 6:18). Missionaries will face temptations that were never expected. Only through the power of the Spirit and in watchfulness and prayer can we experience freedom from sin and spiritual growth in grace. Sinful as we are, enough iniquity

---

6   *The Bible Sense Lexicon*, s.v. *"gregoreo,"* https://ref.ly/logos4/Senses?Key-Id=ws.be+become+awake.v.01.

remains in our prayers to condemn us, as Spurgeon so elo-
quently states:

> If in prayer I come before a throne of grace, then the
> faults of my prayer will be overlooked. In beginning
> to pray, dear friends, you feel as if you did not pray.
> The groanings of your spirit, when you rise from
> your knees are such that you think there is nothing
> in them. What a blotted, blurred, smeared prayer
> it is. Never mind; you are not come to the throne
> of justice, else when God perceived the fault in the
> prayer he would spurn it—your broken words, your
> gaspings, and stammerings are before a throne of
> grace. When any one of us has presented his best
> prayer before God, if he saw it as God sees it, there
> is no doubt he would make great lamentation over
> it; for there is enough sin in the best prayer that was
> ever prayed to secure its being cast away from God.
> But it is not a throne of justice I say again, and here
> is the hope for our lame, limping supplications.[7]

But when we seek God in private prayer knowing who we
are and what he can give us regarding our progressive sanctification, he will faithfully give more than we expect to grow us
in our holiness.

Soak in the words of Martyn Lloyd-Jones concerning
prayer:

> We tend to think of sin as we see it in rags and in the
> gutters of life. We look at a drunkard, poor fellow,
> and we say there is sin. That is sin. But that is not
> the essence of sin. To have a real picture and a true
> understanding of sin, you must look at some great
> saint, some unusually devout and devoted man.
> Look at him there on his knees in the very presence
> of God. Even there self is intruding itself and the

---

7   Charles Haddon Spurgeon, "The Throne of Grace," in The Metropolitan
Tabernacle Pulpit Sermons, vol. 17 (London: Passmore & Alabaster, 1871), 679.

temptation for him is to think about himself. To think pleasantly and pleasurably about himself. And to really be worshiping himself rather than God.[8]

As important as it is, our primary goal is not to preach the gospel, nor is it to train believers in Christian doctrine. Our number one goal is our sanctification: "For this is the will of God, your sanctification" (1 Thess. 4:3). If our continual sanctification is God's will, we must ask specifically for this in our prayers—it is vital for the Christian life. To glorify God is to be alone with him in prayer and fall on our face in worship. What good are we for gospel efforts if we do not meet alone with God for the sake of our holiness? The only way missionaries will flee from temptation and sin is through alertness in devoting ourselves to the work of prayer. So easily we forget that to live in the presence of God is to have a life of prayer. Sinclair Ferguson said it well: "We make the great mistake of putting the cart before the horse. Our thinking is: I will pray if I feel like praying. Then, when I feel more like praying, perhaps I will pray with great regularity. But that is not the pattern of biblical experience."[9]

The mission field is dangerous. It is dangerous because Satan does not want us there. He hates the gospel and wants to destroy everything concerning its work. He also wants to destroy our fellowship with God. Therefore, we must be alert; we must be in constant readiness. Missionaries tend to forget that an enemy is in the camp. He is clever and can deceive the servant of God into sin. So, if this enemy hates our message, hates God and us, and wants to destroy everything in his path concerning spiritual growth in Christ, then why would we not draw from our side the weapon of prayer to "stand against the schemes of the devil" (Eph. 6:11)?

---

8   David Martyn Lloyd-Jones, quoted in MacArthur, *Alone with God*, 35.
9   Sinclair B. Ferguson, *Grow in Grace* (Carlisle, PA: Banner of Truth, 1989), 105.

Neglecting prayer is not simply to "give no opportunity to the devil" (Eph. 4:27); neglecting prayer is to let the enemy run rampant through our camp. When we neglect to pray, we give sin ample opportunity to creep into our souls unnoticed. I have seen missionaries on the field consumed with commanding the devil to do this or that, thinking that God honors and answers this kind of prayer. I have seen missionaries tell God that their trial, suffering, or problem is all from the devil and in the name of Jesus command it to go away. When I refer to prayer alone with God, I do not mean that kind of praying, which is bad theology and will never cure the problem. I am talking about meeting with God alone, watching, placing your face to the ground in worship, covering your hands and your feet, begging God to keep you pure, holy, righteous, sinless, and asking to be "filled with the knowledge of his will in all spiritual wisdom and understanding, so as to walk in a manner worthy of the Lord" (Col. 1:9–10). The only way to be "strong in the Lord and in the strength of his might" (Eph. 6:10) is to pray like this, alert, alone in our inner room, for the benefit of our souls.

Oh, that we missionaries would never forsake the delightful duty of sweet prayer with our Lord. Our lives depend on it. Not only do we have a ruthless enemy but we also have our flesh to battle every day. And we will lose the fight with our flesh if we do not forsake ourselves and our wants and seek our Lord in private communion, beseeching him for his help and grace to keep us holy. We will become restless, antsy, fatigued, and emotional when it comes to praying intimately with God, but we must take heart. He is omnipotent and will help us in our intense and agonizing prayers concerning our spiritual state. Missionaries, please remember your sanctification in holiness will only be won through constant intimate prayer alone with God.

The Blessing of Our Ministry

The second reason to be alone with God in prayer is for the blessing of our ministry. Tribes have been converted because missionaries were on their knees begging God to save them.

Do we commit time to the Lord in prayer for the people we are serving? Are their eternal souls so important to us that we will go to God's throne on their behalf? Why go around the world to proclaim the gospel, treat the sick, help the poor, but never once go in prayer to the only person who can do the work of regeneration and justification? How terrible to neglect to ask the King, with all his authority and power, to save dead sinners from their sins and give them life eternal. Why would we not long for this time in secret (like we long for other earthly duties) to plead to our loving God for this exemplary work of salvation?

The best example of a heart that thought this way is apostle and missionary Paul, whose "heart's desire and prayer to God for them is that they may be saved" (Rom. 10:1). In fact, we find the true depths of Paul's heart in the previous chapter, where we see and feel his distress over his kinsmen. He writes, "I am speaking the truth in Christ—I am not lying; my conscience bears me witness in the Holy Spirit—that I have great sorrow and unceasing anguish in my heart. For I could wish that I myself were accursed and cut off from Christ for the sake of my brothers, my kinsmen according to the flesh" (Rom. 9:1–3).

Several words stand out in these three verses. First, Paul says he has "great sorrow and unceasing anguish" (v. 2). The word Paul uses for "sorrow" is the Greek word *lype*. This word means "pain of mind or spirit, grief, emotional sorrow, and affliction."[10] Jesus used the same word when speaking to his disciples in John 16:6: "But because I have said these things to you, *sorrow* has filled your heart" (emphasis added). An emotional sadness is involved with this word. I often wonder how many tears Paul shed for his spiritually dead kinsmen.

The other word he uses is *anguish*, from the Greek word *odyne*, which means "a feeling of mental pain and distress."[11]

---

10   *The Bible Sense Lexicon*, s.v. "*lype*," https://ref.ly/logos4/Senses?KeyId=ws. sadness.n.01.

11   *The Bible Sense Lexicon*, s.v. "*odyne*," https://ref.ly/logos4/Senses?KeyId=ws. suffering.n.04.

Paul is saying, "I have great sadness, plus mental and physical pain, for my countrymen because they are without Christ."

At this point, Paul wishes something on himself. He says that he wishes he "were accursed and cut off from Christ" for the sake of his kinsmen (v. 3). The words *accursed* and *cut off* are one and the same but gain even more emotional charge as we read them. We see Paul's heart go from severe sadness and pain to wishing a curse upon himself. To wish that he were accursed from Christ shows the depths of his love for his countrymen. The word *curse* is the Greek word *anathema*. It is the same word he uses in Galatians 1:9: "As we have said before, so now I say again: If anyone is preaching to you a gospel contrary to the one you received, let him be accursed [*anathema*]." Paul is expressing that he is in so much pain for his countrymen, he will accept eternal damnation for their eternal salvation—a separation from Christ that is eternal.

At the same time, he continually prayed for their salvation (Rom. 10:1). His mind, body, and soul met God in deep anguishing prayer for the rescue of his kinsmen. As missionaries, is our heart's desire so much in love with God and the people we serve that we would pour ourselves out in intense and agonizing prayer that weeps and moans for their lost souls to be saved? If we are honest, we do not think in terms of being *anathema* for the people we are called to serve. But our love for them should reach to its pinnacle, just like Paul's love in Romans 9.

Missionaries preparing to go and those already on the field have a common tendency to place the missionary life into one category—namely, we go to preach the gospel. We easily fall into the danger of viewing prayer as a secondary category in mission work. Although preaching the gospel is the main reason we are sent to the field, most of the time, we do not think of prayer as being on the same level. It is almost as if we view gospel preaching and prayer as separate ministries. This is dangerous because that type of thinking can separate the gospel and prayer as one being more important than the other. We should never view these two means of grace as separate.

In Scripture, preaching the gospel is coupled with fervent prayer—they go hand in hand. Luke writes, "And they devoted themselves to the apostles' teaching and the fellowship, to the breaking of bread and the prayers" (Acts 2:42). Also, Paul says, "For everything created by God is good, and nothing is to be rejected if it is received with thanksgiving, for it is made holy by the word of God and prayer" (1 Tim. 4:4–5). God is pleased to work his good news in the hearts of sinners through the preached Word, but also through prayer as we ask that they would receive the Word, and therefore, repent and believe. The mark of true missionaries is found in their labors in prayer within their inner room being fully alert to what Christ has done for them and can do for the dead sinners they serve. Being alone with God, watchful in prayer, in a closet with the door locked, will heap upon us eternal rewards, both now and in heaven. "For the eyes of the Lord are on the righteous, and his ears are open to their prayer" (1 Peter 3:12).

Praying with Your Family

In 2010, I was traveling to churches across the United States to share my passion for preaching the gospel to the Korowai people in Papua. My travels took me to the HeartCry office to meet the staff and discuss potential opportunities to work together in Indonesia. As the conversations went on, the subject turned to prayer. One of the men, now a dear friend, looked at me intently and said, "There are plenty of boys on the mission field doing ministry and wrapped up in so many things and yet are neglecting their families. Be a man; pray with your wife and pray with your children." This conversation continued for quite a while because this man had such strong convictions about the husband praying alone with his wife and the family praying together. I left that discussion encouraged, exhorted, and moved in my soul to heed these words.

Have I been faithful since that time to pray every day with my wife and children? No, and I do not think any missionary—or man, for that matter—can answer yes. Every husband can see his need to be more faithful in prayer with his bride and children. As a husband, I am still learning to be faithful in praying with my wife several times a day. Committing to pray together takes work. Why do missionaries yearn and labor so hard in the ministry to serve other people and yet neglect the delightful responsibility of praying with their own flesh?

What do I mean by "own flesh"? Genesis 2:24 says, "Therefore a man shall leave his father and his mother and hold fast to his wife, and they shall become *one flesh*" (emphasis added). Scripture makes it clear that the husband and wife are one. Jesus quotes Genesis 2:24 in Matthew 19:5: "And the two shall become one flesh." Jesus goes deeper in this text and says, "So they are no longer two but one flesh" (v. 6). The husband and wife are one body, one person. God no longer sees them as two, but one. If we take this to heart and apply it to the man's leadership toward his wife concerning prayer, we are left not with one forsaking the other but with one-half leading the whole. Missionary husbands must adore their spouses so much that to neglect to pray with their wives would be to not care about their own bodies, especially their spiritual well-being.

One way you love your wife as yourself is to dive deep into sacred prayer with the Lord, who will bless your marriage and be pleased to make you, as one flesh, dwell in his chambers with sweet communion. Your relationship will grow and be blessed. God will reward you as you seek him in prayer as a couple. If you have not been praying as a couple, then it will feel awkward at first, especially for the husband, because you are seeking to find the words that will put you out of your comfort zone. No missionary husband finds it awkward to pray with anyone outside their own home, but when it comes to their own flesh, it feels different. But that can change. Seek to pray with your wife. Lead her in all righteousness, and you will find that your relationship as one will shine brighter and sweeter in love for one another and for the Lord Jesus Christ. Your wife needs to know what you struggle with. You need to know what she struggles with. You must learn how to pray for her and she for you. Remember, you are one body. No longer are you two.

You must be whole and complete, and that will only happen when the husband leads his own body in prayer to God.

Family Worship

Many men have written about family worship, but I have never been more moved than when I heard Dr. Joel Beeke preach on this subject. My thinking as a husband and father changed concerning our worship to God as a family. Dr. Beeke clearly argued from Scripture that prayer for the family is done through the leadership of the husband and father. I was so radically impacted that I went home and implemented family worship every evening.

Why is family worship so important? It allows fathers to teach and pray with their children. As missionary fathers, do we spend time in prayer with our families? Are we teaching our children how to pray? Do we meet as families at the altar of God and pour out our souls to him for our spiritual benefit? Our families need to see our heart for God. They need to see our tears for the sake of holiness, both for them and for ourselves. If there was ever a day that we need men to lead their families through prayer, it is today.

Life on the mission field is difficult. One of the things you will face in your ministry is whether you should cut an activity out of your schedule or avoid something so that you can lead your family in worship. It will hit you like a ton of bricks—trust me. Many times, I wanted to collapse at 6:00 p.m. because I had not sat down all day due to ministry duties. But 6:00 p.m. is family time. You are at home, it is evening, your wife and children are surrounding you, and what a shame it would be to forsake their spiritual progress to take a siesta. I know the difficulties of the mind and body during those times.

Serving on the mission field is not an excuse for neglecting our own flesh and blood. We must get past the thinking that puts the ministry in the center and the family in the corner. This is not God's design, even for ministers of the gospel. Pray with your children. Let your tears flow for Christ and for their souls, and they will see a man who walks with God. Your wife and children will know they have a husband and a father who loves them and their eternal state before the living God. They will see a man who is dependent on God and learn to do the same for themselves.

Missionaries must be people of prayer. It is your most eminent necessity. You must always be alert, going into your inner room, locking the door, and being alone with Christ for the sake of your sanctification and the salvation and spiritual growth of those you teach. You must pray with your spouse, filling her soul with spiritual meat that will only turn out to be a reward for you both. Lead your family in prayer. Teach your children to obey the commands of Scripture that teach us to "pray without ceasing" (1 Thess. 5:17), and the Holy Spirit will reward you beyond your wildest expectations.

A Challenge to the Sending Church and Mission Organization

Churches and mission organizations have a huge responsibility in sending missionaries. With every missionary you confirm and commission, how many do you teach and encourage concerning their prayer life? Churches are quick to check on a missionary's eschatology but never on his prayer time with God. Over the course of my ministry, only two people have asked me about my prayer habits and how I was doing in this regard.

Local sending church, you have the greatest responsibility because you are the driving force behind your missionary. The mission organization is there to assist and help you in your goals for gospel efforts through your missionary. So, what have you implemented in your missionaries' lives concerning prayer? Can you as a church say, without a shadow of a doubt, that your missionaries understand and are committed to the commands in Scripture regarding their prayer lives?

You are likely focused on the external, the results, what people will hear from the missionary's mouth. You focus on their funds and how much they need and on their extra required training. All these things are needed and good. God forbid you send a missionary untrained and ill-equipped. But something is missing in all this preparation. Are you teaching, encouraging, and building a solid foundation for your missionary's private prayer life? Do not think that this discipline comes naturally or that missionaries can handle this aspect of their spiritual discipline on their own.

The disciples, who walked with Jesus and were taught by him, asked, "Lord, teach us to pray, as John taught his disciples" (Luke 11:1). And Jesus taught them how to pray, to be persistent in prayer, and to ask, ask, ask. If the disciples asked for help in prayer, what makes us think we are in better shape in this area? Are you helping and teaching your missionary in this biblical principle? They cannot survive on the field without an understanding and knowledge of the importance of personal prayer. What are you doing, church, to spur on action in the doctrine of prayer? If your missionary is already on the field, you must proactively encourage and disciple them to see their need for private prayer with their God. Ask them.

The local sending church can do two primary things for your missionary's spiritual edification. First, the church body must pray without ceasing for their missionaries. You have sent them into war, to face an enemy that is clever and dangerous. Pray for them in your worship services, small groups, and other activities. Ask God to show them the urgency of their need to go into their closet and lock the door for prayer. This is crucial. Missionaries worldwide are experiencing a crisis—a lack of understanding and urgency for private prayer. Not all are like this, but most. Develop a special prayer team at your church for your missionaries. They can keep in touch with the missionary and check on prayer requests.

Second, the church elders must continually teach, disciple, and mentor their missionaries to daily exercise private prayer for the spiritual well-being of their souls, their families, and the people they serve. Whether by video chat or spending time with them in person, ask them directly, "Are you spending time alone with God in study and prayer?" If they answer no, then steps need to be taken to come alongside them for their progressive sanctification. Ministry duties can wait. Missionaries must see their dire need for private Bible study and prayer. It is not healthy to neglect such excellent disciplines. Go for broke in nurturing and discipling your missionaries. I have seen too much distance on the field between the church and the missionary. It is time for a change.

As a mission organization, your role is to support the sending church. Work side by side to see that this church is succeeding in its desire for unreached peoples. What should this look like?

When I first joined a mission organization years ago (I am not with an organization anymore but am now solely sent out by my church), I was put through several tests to check my Bible knowledge, doctrine, and how I would proclaim the gospel to a lost person. I did this in front of many people. However, there was never a time during the candidate schooling when I was asked about my prayer life. Why? Is this an embarrassing question? Do people feel uncomfortable asking about this? You bet they do, and I know why. It is because the missionary usually replies, "It could be better," or "I do not really know." If a missionary responds this way, it may indicate that he needs to spend more time alone with God in prayer. When you ask someone, "How is your private prayer life before God?" and they respond, "I see my need because of how great a sinner I am, and I can do nothing without being dependent on my Lord," praise God, right? The sad reality is we rarely if ever hear that kind of response.

Mission organization, much work is needed to spiritually equip missionaries on the field. They must see their need to win the battle for holiness. In your training through the local sending church, show them their need. Show them with full conviction that their lives depend on it. Do check their doctrine, but also check their prayer life. Teach them, show them, and groom them in this heavenly arena of prayer. Your task in

preparing your missionary is far bigger than perhaps you realize, but the eternal rewards will outweigh the labors you invest.

Father in heaven, you are worthy of all worship. You have commanded us to be in constant prayer because you are the only
one who can sanctify us and make us like yourself.

Father, you love us with an everlasting love as your sons and
daughters who you have called to proclaim your gospel to unreached peoples. Help us in this most noble task to commit ourselves to fervent prayer, asking with full assurance according to
your will that you will answer because you are a giving God. You
gave us saving faith through your Son, Jesus Christ. May we as
missionaries pattern our lives after his.

May missionary men and women not subject themselves to ministry duties only but place the highest value on intimate prayer
with you. May each missionary pray for holiness before you.
May each missionary pray for the people he or she now serves
for the gospel. Please, heavenly Father, change us. Show us the
need for prayer and how to pray. May husbands lead their wives
and their families in prayer because we are dependent on you
and you alone.

We ask this for the glory of your name, so that you increase and
we decrease. Amen.

4

Drowning in Unaccountability

As usual, it was stifling hot in Danowage. Every afternoon between 1:00 and 3:00 p.m., we stay inside because of the extreme heat. But on this day, against my better judgment, I was outside helping Jimmy repair some rotted floorboards on his porch during these hot hours. Jimmy is one of the Dani evangelists. Just as I was coming to the realization that my sweat rag was so soaked that it was no longer effective, a piercing screech came from the large river beside our house. Alarmed at the panic in the voice, we dropped our tools and ran toward the sound, plunging barefoot through knee-deep mud, sweating profusely, straining through the thick air to reach this person. All we heard over and over was "They are drowning!"

Ahead of me, Jimmy was in a full sprint, wading through mud one moment and scrambling over hot, sharp rocks the next. I was already limping from running barefoot on the rocks and barely kept up. As we ran, which felt like forever because the accident was downriver, I prayed that no one had drowned. After a few minutes, we reached the bank and saw that a Dani boat, carrying eight people and their possessions, had flipped over as it was making a turn in the river. Jimmy immediately asked where everyone was and if they were safe. I was so pumped with adrenaline that I was ready to dive into the dark depths of the river to search for bodies, but praise the Lord, everyone made it to shore safely. The only things at the bottom of the river were the boat engine and a few belongings.

We helped the remaining Dani women to shore and swam in to retrieve some of their personal possessions. They were all shaken but thankful to be alive. Even though they live near water, most Dani people do not know how to swim, which makes it dangerous for them to be on the river. God was merciful to them that day. I walked back to the house with a sigh of relief and feeling comforted knowing that God had saved them from drowning. If need be, Jimmy and I would have risked our lives to save them also.

I have seen missionaries who are sinking and need someone to save them. What do I mean? Many missionaries are drowning in unaccountability. They are not responsible to or consistently held accountable by leadership to justify and explain their actions. If I were to stop writing now and leave you with that statement, would it be enough to create concern and cause you to question what should be done about this problem?

Missionaries can drown in many types of water. Many flounder for lack of pastoral care, others for lack of biblical teaching. Some are smothered in sexual sin, some in other specific sins. A number sink in depression, others in sickness. They drown because no one cares for them, because their sending church has perhaps forgotten what it means to "come alongside" them through pastoral care, or because their mission organization has established so many restrictions that they feel choked. They drown in too much work, in mental and physical breakdown, in losing support. They drown in a lack of love for their Lord, in loneliness and isolation, in the overwhelming pressures of ministry. They drown because they are afraid, because they have no one to talk to who understands their situation. They drown because their marriage is not healthy, because their children are rebelling, or because they feel forgotten by their supporters, family, friends, and home churches.

Many have left the field because they were engulfed in one of these situations. All they needed to be rescued from these treacherous waters was someone to sprint barefoot through knee-deep mud to rescue them with no thought but for their safety and well-being. Just as Jimmy and I were ready to dive into dangerous depths to pull people out, so must be the heart attitude of the sending church and mission organization when it comes to the missionary. I will not mince words in this chapter because this is heavy on my heart.

This crisis of accountability on the field stems from two important factors that the church and the mission agency have overlooked or forgotten. First, sending churches and mission organizations have lost connection with what missionaries face. Exceptions exist, of course; not all churches and mission organizations have turned their backs regarding missionary accountability, not every missionary is willing to listen to reproof, and other circumstances play a role as well. But the sad reality is that many sending churches and mission organizations have left their missionaries to fend for themselves, and they have done so because they are simply ignorant of the trials, problems, and difficulties missionaries face. Second, these entities have forgotten that missionaries are sinners just like anyone else. Yes, missionaries have Christ's imputed righteousness credited to them through his person and work, and the Holy Spirit has regenerated them, but they are still susceptible to sin—weak, frail, and in danger of drowning in any of the waters mentioned, just like any other believer. Churches and mission organizations must awaken to their responsibility in this arena of accountability and act upon it.

This chapter discusses several essential areas where missionaries are drowning in unaccountability so that the church and the mission organization can successfully hold them accountable. Sending churches and mission organizations have a lot to learn, just like the missionaries they send, who must move to new cultures and deal with life in third-world countries.

When my sending church first commissioned and sent us to Papua, Indonesia, we were the first they had ever sent. The leadership admitted they were new at this and had much to learn. That confession benefited me because I knew they wanted to do things right as we represented them on the field. Have they done everything right? No. No church, mission organization, or missionary will ever do anything perfectly. What is important is their heart's desire spurring them to growth and biblical action for the sake of their missionaries.

As a missionary for more than ten years, let me describe what happens from the time a new missionary and his family are commissioned until he is drowning in the depths of unaccountability. As you read this, know that these are stories from various missionaries, including myself. I have observed missionaries over the last ten years and have combined these accounts to give a detailed depiction of reality.

The Missionary's Reality

A missionary who has the desire to move overseas and preach the gospel exudes excitement. He is being discipled and mentored by his sending church, growing in the Scriptures, and progressing in his spiritual life. He travels to other churches preaching the Word, giving presentations, and sharing about his mission organization that is committed to taking the gospel to the unreached and disengaged. Hopefully, his passion sounds forth with unstoppable force.

Those listening feel compelled to support him and his family because they see his willingness to give up everything and live however necessary for the spread of the gospel. The church leadership sees someone who is devoted to the Word and has the gift of preaching and teaching. They meet with him to check his doctrine and life for potential partnership. If that goes well, the church votes. They send their monthly support check to either his sending church or mission organization, committing to spread the gospel to this unreached people group.

The missionary continues preaching, presenting, meeting new people, and talking long hours at other churches. These churches are truly interested and want to be involved. They want to hear about the people group, get to know the missionary and his family, and discuss missions. The missionary is excited to do this but nervous at the same time—he is being watched, questioned, observed, and evaluated nonstop.

"If you need anything, at any time, call us." "What can we do for you?" "I could not do what you do—you are amazing." "You are my hero, thank you for going." "Let me wash your feet." The comments go on and on, and the missionary politely smiles and says, "Thank you." People are sincere and mean well. Sometimes the comments encourage; other times they add the heavy pressure of expectation to a missionary's already-full plate.

Because the task of raising support is enormous, the missionary often wonders if he will ever get to the field. He trusts and believes that one day he will. He prays, "Lord, I have theological studies, a family to lead and support, a full-time job, other training to do, and I need to raise between $50,000 and $80,000 to serve there. Please help!"

Three years later, if the missionary has been diligent, the hard work and prayers have paid off, and the missionary finally has his support. He has finished Bible school, linguistic training, cross-cultural training, and medical training. His church has been by his side mentoring, grooming, and discipling him throughout the process. He has had sweet fellowship with his church and other believers. Excitedly, with thrills in his soul, he sends out his final stateside update. He says goodbye to family and friends, not knowing if he will ever see them again. The fifty-two-hour plane ride to a new land feels like an eternity. He is ready; his wife is ready. Once they hit the ground, they will dive into cultural and language learning.

A couple of intense months later, after they are settled, he writes his first update from the field. But something is wrong. He has had dysentery for six weeks. Diarrhea has become a daily activity, and he is frequently doubled over in pain. His clothes hang loosely and his energy lags. He has missed much of his language learning because of sickness. At one point, a friend drove him to the hospital on a motorbike in the pouring rain holding a stool sample to give to the doctor. His wife has *giardia*, which recurs every other week.[1] She is unhappy with her new surroundings. The kids are being disobedient and having cultural adjustment problems, while Dad and Mom are away in language class, when their stomachs permit them. The mosque speakers beside the house blare the *sholat* five times a day.[2] Reality has set in. What have I done?

Unwilling to express his true emotions and feelings, which would reveal how difficult things are, he pens a vague update. He wants supporters to see him as a fighter, a go-getter for the gospel, a bold person with a John Wayne–type grit to move forward because he worries, "If the church sees my struggles and difficulties, they will question their commitment to me and may drop their support." A superman missionary is birthed in the eyes of his churches because all they receive is a vague update. They see everything as perfect and think this man is a "true missionary."

Months and years have passed. The missionary's sending church has not contacted him. His mission organization is only concerned with managing his finances. So far, the organization has offered no hand of fellowship in the form of pastoral care or personal interaction. With disappointment and self-loathing, he realizes the romance is dead and the excitement to live with a new people is gone. He blames himself for the fact that the

---

1   *Giardiasis* is a protozoan infection that causes watery diarrhea, churning stomach, abdominal pain, and occasionally vomiting. It is usually found in contaminated food or drinking water or can be passed from person to person. Vanderkooi, *The Village Medical Manual*, 219–220.

2   *Sholat* is the Indonesian word for prayer. In Islam, *sholat* refers to the five daily prayers that are an integral part of this religion. See http://islam4muslims. weebly.com/sholat.html.

smells, people, noises, city, jungle, heat, sicknesses, drunks, fights, and constant repairs are starting to irritate him. He cannot stand being around the people he has been sent to serve. He hides when he hears them approach his door, and as he does, he hates himself more, thinking often, "What have I done?"

He has not been reading the Bible as much as he should. He is battling for joy. His private prayer with the Lord is dwindling. Family worship is once a month, if that. Sundays have grown stale because he has no fellowship with other believers or solid biblical teaching. His heart is beginning to show signs of coldness and a lack of caring. Family life is stressful, and now another update is due to his supporters. He writes again. This time, hints of a struggle show between the lines, but it is still vague. He is embarrassed at how things have become. He sees himself as a failure because he has not been studying the Bible or praying as much as he knows he should. He fights for energy and spiritual strength. He recalls all the times people told him how great he was or said, "You are amazing—I could not do what you are doing."

Finally, his heart in turmoil, he writes again to his supporters, yet he does not tell the churches or his mission organization that he is drowning spiritually and physically. He writes about the successes and shows great pictures. To the church and mission organization, things seem to be progressing well. He sends regular updates and gets emails from various people. They tell him he is very special and that they are praying for him and his family, and they ask where they can send extra funds for particular ministry needs he has written about.

Only five churches out of thirty contact him to say they are praying for him and the family. He never hears from his sending church or mission organization, and yet he labors on, serving the people, teaching the Scriptures, and helping the sick, all the while forgetting his own soul. Have they forgotten me?

In desperate need of a respite, he and his family visit the expat church in the city, expecting to hear solid Bible teaching, but the speaker is showing movie scenes to make his point.

This discouragement continues for four or five years or more. He is fighting for joy and missing sweet fellowship and biblical teaching. Things begin to pile up, and each day he is reminded that the stresses of life multiply ten times on the field. If only someone had warned him of that before he arrived.

He tries to keep his family in order and feed himself, but he feels cold and defeated, burned out from all his labors. Recurring sickness has depleted his energy and ability to serve like he used to. He feels alone. Ministry has become so busy and difficult, and the thought of quitting crosses his mind, bringing with it guilt and self-doubt. He is at odds with his teammates or has not seen them in several years because they are in the States trying to heal from sickness. His sending church is still silent. His mission organization is disconnected from his situation on the field. He and his field director are not getting along because of the leadership wanting total control of his ministry, and their meetings do not go well. Weariness overwhelms him. What am I to do?

Another update is due. What to say? How to say it? Depression consumes him, but he does not want the churches to see him as a failure because, after all, they have spoken so highly of him and invested funds. They expect his unreached people group to respond to the gospel. What can he write? He crafts another update showing the progress in the ministry and includes tons of pictures, but he never openly speaks of his own soul or the state of his family. He uses language that is all too common and avoids the gut-wrenching truth. He sends the update and receives a few polite responses, but nothing changes.

No one is coming. No one is running through the knee-deep mud to rescue him—not from his church; not from his organization. He is drowning in spiritual depression and loneliness and feeling like a total disaster, an utter failure. Will help ever arrive?

The Importance of Fellowship

All missionaries could confess they have lived through at least a few aspects of this deadly spiral. Some more severe than others, but every missionary at some point faces spiritual and physical battles. I have endured times that were so severe I truly thought there was no hope of rescue. This is a real crisis on the mission field that the church and the mission organization must address.

What is most striking in the example you just read? You might note how the missionary's condition evolved, which is remarkable. But the missionary, the church, and the mission organization need to understand what is at the heart of this example—a lack of accountability.

Neither the missionary's sending church nor the mission organization kept up regular communication with him. He was not accountable to either entity. It is as if he was thrown into the vast sea of unreached peoples to fend for himself. Lack of accountability will cause the missionary's spiritual life, family life, and ministry to flounder and eventually sink, whereas regular accountability and support will help these things stay afloat and even flourish.

We dare not give our children a cell phone or computer, allow them to shut the door, and trust that they will stay away from what they should not look at. We would be setting them up for failure and tremendous sin. When we allow our children to use these devices, we install accountable controls to keep them safe. We monitor their activity and limit their time.

"Well," you might say about the missionary, "he is a grown man and was commissioned for this kind of life. He is at fault, right? He needs to pull himself up by his bootstraps and study the Bible and pray more." Missionaries are responsible for their behavior before God just as all believers are, but this is not the correct response. The Christian life is not meant to be lived without fellowship, ongoing discipleship, and spiritual influence. We see this exemplified in Acts 2:42: "They devoted themselves to the apostles' teaching and the fellowship." The first church in Jerusalem was instilled with the importance of fellowship. The word *fellowship* is the Greek word *koinonia*. Its root word, *koinos*, means "common." How does that relate to fellowship? Well, it means they had several things in common.

First, they shared in their relationship with God. Second, they gave to other believers in need. The verse indicates that this was not a onetime sharing and giving but was continual to meet the needs of the brethren. If we apply that same *koinonia* to the missionary life, we find a need that must be met. The missionary needs pastoral care in biblical instruction and fellowship. When a person has godly fellowship with other believers, he can grow and be challenged in his daily Christian life. If there is no fellowship with like-minded believers, then he is set up to struggle in his ongoing sanctification.

The church often forgets that fellowship is essential for missionaries. Pastors who daily shepherd their own flocks do not lack fellowship with like-minded believers. In fact, they can have regular encouragement and accountability from men in the church. Why would it be any different for the missionary? Missionaries are not super-spiritual beings who never have spiritual battles, nor do they possess a spiritual discipline that surpasses everyone else's.

It is not that the missionary does not want to "pursue righteousness, godliness, faith, love, steadfastness, gentleness" and "fight the good fight of the faith" (1 Tim. 6:11–12). He desires to "keep a close watch" on himself and "on the teaching" (1 Tim. 4:16); to "guard the deposit entrusted" to him (1 Tim. 6:20); and to present himself to God "as one approved, a worker who has no need to be ashamed, rightly handling the word of truth" (2 Tim. 2:15). However, fellowship and accountability are vital for missionaries to grow and excel in these areas. The writer of Hebrews speaks about fellowship because in our flesh, we are weak and dependent on "encouraging one another" (Heb. 10:25). Missionaries need the church and the mission organization to act out Philippians 2:4: "Let each of you look not only to his own interests, but also to the interests of others." What does this look like practically?

Drowning from a Lack of Pastoral Care

Over the years, one danger I have observed is a lack of pastoral care for the missionary's soul. What is pastoral care? It is a modern two-word way of describing a pastor/elder shepherding a member of his flock through spiritual counsel, biblical preaching and teaching, emotional/mental counsel, and fellowship.

Many missionaries drown because they do not receive spiritual counsel through biblical teaching that is directed at them for the care of their souls. Many leave the field because they drowned without fellowship, biblical teaching, and encouragement—without pastoral care. I have seen missionaries labor for years, and on the surface, all looks well, but deep in their hearts lies a spiritually festering wound that needs attention through pastoral care.

Too many missionaries sit through boring field meetings week after week, endure shallow teaching on Sundays, deal with the stresses of living abroad that seem to multiply, and still all appears well, but the satisfaction of their souls is not grounded in right, passionate love for God and man as it once was. Some fall into sin and leave the field. Why? They were not held accountable through pastoral care. The sending church and mission organization saw no urgency to continue their discipleship.

You may think, "The missionary is responsible for his own sinful actions." Yes, missionaries must watch and pray so that they do not enter into temptation (Matt. 26:41). It is God himself who keeps us from all sin, not any man. But are missionaries above the spiritual status of King David? He was a man after God's own heart (1 Sam. 13:14), yet he entered into temptation under the efficacy of sin.

The missionary is just a man, like David, and needs spiritual and biblical accountability to keep his heart pure from condemnation and from a guilty conscience before God and man; he is weak and must always be on guard. Part of that guarding comes from accountability through pastoral care. John Owen wrote, "For ourselves, we are weakness itself . . . do not flatter yourselves that you should hold out; there are secret lusts that lie lurking in your hearts, which perhaps now stir not, which, as soon as any temptation befalls you, will rise, tumultuate, cry, disquiet, seduce, and never give over until they are either killed or satisfied."[3] The missionary is to study and pray regularly so that he does not fall into temptation, but the addition of pastoral care will help destroy any sin lurking in his heart that would threaten his communion with God.

You may believe the missionary should be honest and tell his church or mission organization his thoughts and struggles. It is true; he should be open and truthful to his sending church. I make no excuses on that end. But neither the Christian life nor the missionary life was intended to be lived without pastoral care, which is what holds believers accountable. We are all vulnerable and susceptible to sin and need spiritual care in our lives, especially on the field.

We often forget that one way to prevent the dangers of temptation is to hold the man and woman of God on the mission field accountable before the triune God. At one point on the field, I was extremely discouraged because it seemed that every time I turned around, another missionary was leaving because of sin. I trembled for my own soul and grieved for the others. Sending churches and mission organizations must recognize the reality of what must be done for the missionary's spiritual life.

What about the missionary's coworkers? He and his coworkers should be accountable to one another. True, but many missionaries do not have coworkers. A worrisome trend in some sending organizations is that they do not see teammates as essential. Many missionaries go with the blessing of their sending church and mission organization without first establishing teammates. Or the missionary has teammates, but they are in the States because of sickness or burnout, which can last up to three years or more. In the worst-case scenario, the teammates decide not to return.

---

3   John Owen, *Works of John Owen, Vol. 6: Temptation and Sin*, edited by William H. Goold (Carlisle, PA: Banner of Truth, 1966), 104–105.

An additional problem occurs when a missionary writes a fantastic update, is doing well spiritually, has great teammates, and all appears to be well. The sending church and mission organization often read his update and think, "All is good; we do not need to check on this missionary." False. He and his family still need pastoral care for the continued well-being of their souls.

Every time my family and I came out of the village to rest and resupply, we longed for solid, biblical, expository preaching. I love teaching every Sunday, but I also long to be fed from the Word by other saints who bring the depths of Scripture to light for the edification of my soul and worship to God. Unfortunately, most missionaries who preached at the expat church on the coast were not equipped or trained, which left the missionary community (an average of three hundred missionaries, pilots, translators, teachers, nurses, doctors, information technology specialists, counselors, etc.) in this town suffering from spiritual hunger. The missionary at the pulpit would use most of the sermon time to give a motivational talk or show a video of a US pastor who had bad theology or movie clips to make a practical point. What has happened regarding the preaching of the Word on the mission field? My family and I need that precious time of Bible teaching every week for the edification of our souls. So do you.

Sending churches and mission organizations that are committed to preparing missionaries for the field will see them grow and mature in the faith under such accountability, but then when they reach the field, one of two things may happen: (1) they arrive where a community of missionaries is already working, but there is shallow Bible teaching and little accountability from the field side; or (2) they arrive on a field where they are alone and there is no existing missionary work, no church, no accountability, nothing. Both these examples are dangerous for the missionary and his family. Why? Because the one-on-one accountability, face-to-face discipleship, grooming, mentoring, and fellowship he had during training has come to a sudden stop, and the missionary is on his own.

As I think of my own field and the missionaries serving there, I realize just how many must be drowning from a lack of pastoral care and biblical teaching or from bad theology. Where is the pastoral care to feed missionaries and to say, "All Scripture is breathed out by God and profitable for teaching, for reproof, for correction, and for training in righteousness, that the man of God may be complete, equipped for every good work" (2 Tim. 3:16–17)? Where are the churches and mission organizations whose central goal is the spiritual care of their missionaries? Spiritually starving missionaries will be in shambles in their own ministries. Laymen and missionaries alike need deep biblical doctrine taught to them. A shocking amount of poor theology can enter a missionary community that does not have proper leadership in the Word.

What should the church and mission organization do for missionaries who are drowning in a lack of biblical preaching, accountability, and emotional or spiritual counsel?

The Sending Church

If you are a church that has sent missionaries overseas, I hope you tested and confirmed their giftings and doctrine. But do not be confused about your continuing role in their progressive sanctification. Do not assume your missionary is a sinless super-Christian who has no more need for biblical teaching, discipleship, and preaching than anyone else.

This is a common problem in the church today. We send missionaries out with the view that they are super-spiritual giants and no longer need anyone to teach them about Christian doctrine. We have put them in danger of falling face-first because we place them on a pedestal, as if they are too advanced to be taught and counseled.

I have seen this in my travels. People have the best intentions when they speak. Yet sometimes, they speak too highly of the missionary. They are amazed at his countenance, eloquence, and ability to proclaim the Word of God and are impressed that he would go to this particular people group. They view the missionary as if he is some specially made caliber of a person who God no longer needs to sanctify, that he is complete. Such wrong thinking is an error. The biblical understanding of this missionary is that he is just a man, a sinful man in need of the Holy Spirit's help and power just like the next man.

Do not misread me; it is good for a missionary to challenge, inspire, and motivate people to gospel action and live a holy life before God and man. But despite this, he is still a mere man, a sinner saved through the same means as we: through Christ's imputed righteousness.

Missionaries and their families need ongoing direct account-ability and fellowship with their sending church. They must be held accountable. Not all accountability has a negative focus. The sending church should take action to help them feed their souls and their families' souls—this is positive accountability, making sure they and their families are being properly fed and cared for spiritually.

When is the last time you as a sending church asked your missionary what kind of meat he is receiving from the Word? Aside from his personal devotions or listening to a sermon on YouTube, what kind of fellowship is he receiving from other Christian men who are feeding his soul in the Word so that he can, in turn, look at his Christ, his soul, and his ministry with full biblical conviction and be prepared to battle on in the ministry? When was the last time you as a sending church asked how he is doing spiritually? In my life, I can only think of two men in my church who have asked me this. It is as if Christians are afraid to ask each other how they are doing spiritually. But when we ask, it provides the opportunity for pastoral care, which will take time, wise counsel, listening, and biblical instruction based on the response to the question.

Practical Accountability Instructions for the Church

A church can hold missionaries accountable in several ways. A prerequisite is that the man you have sent is elder qualified. With this in mind, you should treat him like the other elders, who are accountable, have ongoing fellowship, and sit under the Word and worship every week with other believers. Think this way when it comes to the missionary you have sent to a hostile place with no accountability, no fellow Christians, and no fellowship. Is he to endure the Christian life alone? No. Here are six ways to implement a new conviction for holding your missionaries accountable.

First, pray for him and his family daily. Perhaps you already do that. Great, but write (email) to him monthly, even weekly, and tell him this. Ask him what specific things the church can pray for. If he wants to honor God, he will be open with you about his struggles.

Second, call him. Today's technology makes it possible set up a time to video chat with him face to face or hear his voice on a call. Have multiple elders there so fellowship and discipleship can continue. If you have regular elder meetings, make time for this as you would for those. Ask him questions: How he is doing spiritually? Is he in the Word? What struggles does he have? How is he leading his family? How is his wife? Have calls that include her. How are the children? Are he and his family studying the Word together? How is his prayer life? Is he making every effort to stay away from temptation? Questions such as these have accountability written all over them because the last thing either of you want is to see him come home because of something you could have helped prevent. Encourage him. Listen to him. Give godly counsel and instruction.

Third, set up a time for him to speak with the congregation via video. This is a great way for the church to remember their missionaries and be involved with their work and lives. The missionary will feel encouraged and see that he is not forgotten, and this will also edify and speak into the lives of people in his church. Once a month is a good goal to aim for so the congregation can be more active in the gospel efforts to the people group you want to reach. Make it a priority.

Fourth, keep your missionary accountable by installing an accountability program on all devices, computers, iPads, tablets, and cell phones. Perhaps one elder could be responsible for this matter. Why is this important? Missionaries can fall into sin and struggle with pornography and lust simply because they were not held accountable to someone who could see their private life in this area. We are all susceptible to this and must guard our minds and hearts for the glory of God and the gospel efforts on the field. Missionaries are no less prone to temptation than other Christians. My household uses Accountable2You so that my family and I do not commit the sin of lust. Please make this a priority for the spiritual well-being of your missionary.

Fifth, and in my opinion, the most important of all, commit to visit your missionary on the field once a year. Place this in your budget and make it a priority. This is not the age of John Paton. We have so many gifts available to us to keep our missionaries accountable. Even in the most remote places in the world, a church can visit their missionary. I have seen several churches visit the missionary for the sole purpose of fellowship, biblical teaching, biblical counsel, and spending time together. This does much for the missionary's spiritual life, his family, and their ministry. Do not think the missionary is too theologically equipped or spiritual for you to speak into his life. We must get past this type of thinking. Send at least one elder and his wife to minister to them. An elder's wife can do much for the well-being of the missionary's wife. Send three or four people, if possible, perhaps a young person thinking about missions or a deacon, but make sure one of these is an elder. This elder can prepare lessons in the Word to minister to the missionary. I guarantee the missionary would love to sit with his family and let an elder teach them. It is a great opportunity for the church to see the ministry for themselves and love on their missionaries as people. I also guarantee it will benefit the congregation. The elder can give a full report when he returns.

Sixth, the missionary and the elders must decide about furloughs. These are vital. Speaking from personal experience, a missionary needs to step away from the work every three years, at minimum. Why? The missionary needs to return to his home church to be refreshed and to rest. All churches must understand the importance of allowing ample time for the missionary to rest. On my first furlough, my sending church counseled me to take the first two months to rest and worship with the church. This was excellent counsel. The missionary needs to debrief with his church, rest, worship, and then travel to his partner churches. The notion of jumping off the plane and traveling across the United States to visit other churches and individuals is unhealthy. The missionary needs time to enjoy his family and sending church and to refresh his soul because furloughs can be tough. While missionaries love to visit partnering churches, being on the road for six months can wear on a person and his family. The missionary needs to start this kind of travel with full energy and feeling refreshed. He and his family may need more than two months with the sending church. Weigh these issues as you talk with your missionary. The missionary needs to hear solid advice for the sake of his family and himself. "Listen to advice and accept instruction, that you may gain wisdom in the future" (Prov. 19:20).

Even on furlough you must not drop your guard in keeping your missionary accountable. When he comes back to the States, this should not mean that you put on hold what you have been doing for him on the field. Keeping your routine will help your missionary stay healthy in his work and spiritual life.

The Mission Organization

Some mission organizations work alongside the missionary's sending church to ensure the missionary is accountable, and they do an excellent job meeting the church's needs regarding the missionary. For those organizations without accountability on their radar, consider how to become what you were designed to be. How may you support a sending church in accountability?

Most mission organizations have a field director and a field leadership team. It is the field leadership's job to facilitate the sending church's work through the missionary. The relationship should never be an authoritarian one in which the field leadership makes demands from the missionary without the sending church's involvement. They should not choke the missionary or the sending church's ministry but help ensure that it progresses according to God's will.

I have seen both scenarios on the field. When a field leadership team is authoritarian and gives the missionary no breathing room (by telling him, for example, "You cannot evangelize in town here while you resupply; you need to focus on the Korowai only"), they have disqualified themselves from the role of holding the missionary accountable. But when the field leadership humbly facilitates the sending church's ministry through the missionary, then they have the right to hold the missionary accountable. When the field director and leadership team line themselves up under the sending church, the missionary is at liberty to be accountable to the leadership on the field because in essence, the leadership team has become an extension of the missionary's sending church. In due time, the sending church and the missionary will be able to see the field leadership's desires, whether positive or negative.

In select cases, a missionary's sending church may be uninvolved in accountability. They may have never learned this or think it does not apply for their missionary. In such situations, the mission organization's duty is to fill in this gap. If the sending church will not resolve to keep the missionary accountable, the mission organization must step in and do so. How should they do this? How can a mission organization with a thousand missionaries or more take on this kind of responsibility?

Practical Accountability Instructions for the Mission Organization

Before the missionary joins your organization, fully explain your policies regarding accountability on the field. Before any missionary signs his name, you should know what he is up against when it comes to his sending church's participation. Be involved in accountability by showing the missionary and his sending church that you will do what is required if the church needs you to act. The following five practical steps will help you, in cooperation with the sending church, keep the missionary accountable.

First, pray for your missionaries daily and ask for specific prayer requests so you can pray more diligently. Call and write emails, but do not just do this for the first month or so and then drop off communication. Make this a discipline because you are dealing with sinners saved through the same means as anyone else. Missionaries face many temptations, trials, and sufferings before and even more so on the field. Show that you do not just care about handling their money but about their souls and their progressive sanctification. We must never minimize prayer. You do not need the sending church's permission to pray and talk with the missionary.

Second, make sure the field directors and leadership team meet regularly with the missionary, but only for prayer, encouragement, and anything the missionary would like to share. Your field leadership must make it clear that they are available anytime they are needed. Too many field meetings have become "my way or the highway" concerning the dos and do nots of ministry. Too many field directors and leadership teams reek of authoritarianism. Do not start off on the wrong foot. Meet to build up the missionary, help him succeed in his gospel efforts, pray with him, and encourage him in the Word of God. In these meetings, ask how he is doing spiritually. If he is struggling, make this a time of building him up with godly counsel rather than reprimanding him, unless the missionary has done something wrong or sinful, in which case he should be rebuked biblically and in love. Remember, you are there to line up under his sending church. Communicate with the church about your meetings. This will build your relationship with both the missionary and his church. Field leadership must give godly counsel and advice in the ministry; however, they must not demand something from the missionary regarding the ministry if the church has not been informed first.

Third, center your field meetings on the Word of God and prayer. I have experienced meetings that choke the life out of everyone in the room because they were not focused on the Bible and prayer. Do not let field meetings drag on with meaningless details. Instead, focus on the Word of God, prayer, and fellowship. Find a man who will teach sound biblical doctrine. Too many opportunities have been wasted because the mission organization invited someone who was unequipped to accurately proclaim the truths of Scripture. One time a pastor came from the United States to a quarterly field meeting. He stood up to preach and told the missionaries that if they drank alcohol to get a buzz, that was a sin. Is that what they needed to hear? No. Missionaries on the field need someone to open the Scriptures and teach them solid, biblical doctrine to encourage their hearts to press on in their faith and in the ministry. They should leave that time of worship seeing Christ as more beautiful than when they came into the meeting. As a mission organization, you are in the business of building missionaries up so that their gospel efforts are carried out with great conviction and zeal.

Fourth, encourage your missionaries to meet and build relationships with other missionaries in your own and other organizations. They could play sports together or meet at a restaurant or coffee shop. If schedules are difficult to work around, meetings can occur through video conferencing. This form of fellowship is vital for missionaries to combat isolation and build one another up. I looked forward to playing basketball with other missionaries on the coast when my family and I came out of the jungle to rest and resupply. These men were facing the same stresses and struggles that I was, and these were opportunities to see my friends and encourage one another in the faith. When believers come together like this, they remember they are not alone in the battle for their sanctification and gospel efforts.

Fifth, make sure the home office and host country are not distant or unresponsive. Send someone from the main office to the field periodically. Because this is for the missionary's sake, do not send someone who will just go sightseeing. Send a husband and wife who are equipped to give godly instruction and who want to spend time with the missionary and his family, a couple who genuinely want to get to know the missionary family and speak into their lives. Once a year is a good frequency to ensure that they are encouraged spiritually. Remember to speak to the sending church about this. The sending church should have communication from you regarding the spiritual accountability of their missionary.

May all this be done for the glory of our Lord so that the missionary can continue to labor in the harshest circumstances and blaze even brighter for Christ's honor and beauty among unreached peoples.

Father in heaven, we submit to you and your sovereignty over us as Lord and Savior and want to honor you in all things, even in our labors for the gospel. Help us, Lord, to realize the importance of accountability in service for your kingdom. We do not want to dishonor your name by sinning before your throne. Help us to be humble in accepting biblical counsel, advice, and teaching so that we can work in the power of the Holy Spirit with a clear conscience before you and man.

Help missionaries to stay accountable before you through godly instruction from others. Keep them from sin. Guard their hearts from the evil one and from their own flesh. Help them to live pure and holy before you so that your gospel can spread to the most unreached places in the world. Your Word teaches that the Christian life is not meant to be lived in isolation, so help missionaries see the importance of this for their souls.

Lord, give your church a conviction to continually lead, disciple, and teach missionaries both before and on the field so that the man of God is equipped and ready for anything, good or evil, that comes his way. Lord, give mission agencies an understanding of their role in the missionary's gospel work. Help them to submit to the local church and be there for the missionary in all matters of spiritual progress.

Let us not fall into temptation, but deliver us from evil, for yours is the kingdom and the power and the glory forever and ever. Amen.

5

The Dangers of Being
a Missionary Family

I remember our first week in Papua in 2009. We traveled to
Indonesia for a month to investigate multiple tribes and locations for our potential gospel efforts. On one occasion, I went
interior with another missionary to survey the lowland swamps
of Papua, and my family stayed in the coastal town with a few
other missionaries. While I was away, my wife Patricia spent
time with the missionary ladies. At a luncheon one afternoon,
she had a conversation about family with the field director's
wife that still stands out to me. But before I tell you what she
said, I want to make clear what my convictions are concerning
the family under the leadership of our heavenly Father.

God's Design

God designed the family to be a miraculous picture of the unity
we see in the Trinity. The Father, Son, and Holy Spirit share
a perfect union in their relationship as three in one. The family
was designed to have the same relationship as the Trinity does
in the gospel. The Trinitarian gospel is preached and taught in

the home first. Then, gospel action moves from the home into the church, which consists of multiple families, and then out into the world. That is why the local church is so important because it is made from family units who are zealous for this Trinitarian gospel to reach the unreached peoples. The church, which is the lifeblood for the family, is the spearhead for gospel advance. Of the family, Pollard and Brown say, "God designed the family to be a living demonstration of various aspects of the glory of the gospel and the embodiment of biblical truths... As Christ's Church is the pillar and ground of the truth, the biblical family can be a biblical preservative of the gospel and a blessed field of evangelism."[1]

When a family lives out Scripture's commands, fulfilling each role according to God's design, then the union and relationship within that family shines like the relationship within the Trinity. Husbands are commanded to love their wives (Eph. 5:25). Wives are commanded to submit to their husbands (Eph. 5:22). Children are commanded to obey their parents in the Lord (Eph. 6:1) and honor their father and mother (Ex. 20:12). Fathers are commanded to "not provoke [their] children to anger, but bring them up in the discipline and instruction of the Lord" (Eph. 6:4). The word *provoke* simply means that fathers should not anger or irritate their children by blaming them harshly or having a temper that causes them to be discouraged. The father is to be the prophet, priest, and king in the home (Eph. 6:4; 1 Tim. 3:4; 1 Peter 2:5, 9). The mothers are to "love their husbands and children, to be self-controlled, pure, working at home, kind, and submissive to their own husbands" (Titus 2:4–5).

The family is God's masterpiece designed to bring him glory and honor and should radiate Christ inside and outside the home. This will only happen when fathers take up their God-given role and commit to obeying Scripture. Soak in the words of J. W. Alexander: "There is no member of a household whose individual piety is of such importance to all the rest, as

---

1   Scott T. Brown and Jeff Pollard, preface to *A Theology of the Family* (Wake Forest, NC: National Center for Family-Integrated Churches, 2014), 36, 40.

the father or head; and there is no one whose soul is so directly influenced by the exercise of domestic worship. Where the head of a family is lukewarm or worldly, he will send the chill through the whole house."[2]

A vital attribute of the family is that the husband and wife are one, not two (Gen. 2:24). There should be no opposition in this unity, the covenant of marriage. The husband does not focus on himself or try to fulfill his own wants and desires. The wife does not seek to make her own choices and lord over her husband. The two have become one, which means they are seeking to work toward the other's good. The husband leads and teaches his wife in all righteousness and vows to place her before himself. The wife gives the role of leadership to the husband and seeks to build him up for the glory of God.

Man's Challenges to God's Design

The world is trying to destroy the family unit. As believers and as missionaries, we must have a clear understanding of how the family works and the importance it plays in cross-cultural missions. Some questions to work through include these: How does the husband/father balance the workload in missions and yet continue to lead and care for his family? What is the role of the wife/mother in the work of missions? Should she be willing to forsake the normalcy of the family unit, whether that means seeing her husband gone all the time or interacting with the people so much that she neglects her family? What do the children need, and how much should the husband and wife sacrifice from their mission work to be godly parents?

The mission field holds many dangers for families, and missionary families have succumbed to several of them. My prayer is that this chapter will help, encourage, and cause husbands, fathers, wives, and mothers on the mission field to reevaluate their lives and determine whether they are or are perhaps close to drowning from the dangers surrounding them.

---

2 James W. Alexander, *Thoughts on Family Worship*, ed. Don Kistler (Grand Rapids: Soli Deo Gloria, 1998), 16–17.

Let me return to what the field director's wife said. Patricia was invited to lunch on the missionary compound by another missionary lady to fellowship with other missionary wives. According to my wife, the conversation was casual at first as the women got to know one another. As they ate, the subject turned to the missionary wife's role in ministry. Several women gave advice, and then the field director's wife said, "Prepare to be without your husband a lot, and prepare to raise your children without him." That was discouraging, and the next comment added to it: "It feels like you are a missionary widow."

As you can probably guess, my wife knew that even though we were committed to a missionary life, I would never place that life above the family. When Patricia shared this interaction with me later, she and I spent time discussing God's design for the family. My wife already knew I did not agree with these women's comments, but it was still beneficial for us to unpack these common beliefs and even pray for these other missionary families who are under the impression that absentee fathers are an unfortunate but expected sacrifice in gospel efforts.

Are you in shock after reading about the all-too-common loss of relationship between husband and wife and between father and children? It saddens me to know some fathers leave, placing ministry work above his family to the point that his wife feels like a widow. Does God bless the family if the husband/father is not around for his wife and children because he is somewhere else fulfilling his ministry wants and responsibilities? In missions, does the Lord command us to be away from our families to the point that wives call themselves "missionary widows"?

I have seen this sad tale firsthand; many missionary husbands/dads are so wrapped up in their gospel work that they neglect the very people God gave them to minister to first. Remember that the gospel starts in the home and works its way to the dark streets of the unreached. It should never be the other way around. Dads should never place their work for the lost, in whatever setting or place, above their families. No, God cannot bless and does not overlook fathers' motives when their gospel work occurs at the expense of neglecting their families. The results are never healthy or positive.

Unfortunately, I have heard several arguments in favor of this type of thinking for cross-cultural missions, that fathers are somehow "off the hook" because they are accomplishing important ministry work. What does Christ command regarding the family and missions?

Leaving the Family for the Sake of the Gospel: Matthew 19 and Luke 18

Regarding this issue, what about Matthew 19:29 or Luke 18:29–30? Here is what Jesus says in Matthew 19:29: "And everyone who has left houses or brothers or sisters or father or mother or children or lands, for my name's sake, will receive a hundredfold and will inherit eternal life."

Comments stemming from this verse include "Jesus rewards those who leave and forsake family for the gospel" and "It is biblical to leave your wife and children for the gospel's sake." But is this what Jesus is teaching here? What is he really saying to Peter after Peter tells him, "See, we have left everything and followed you" (Matt. 19:27)? After all, Peter had a wife.

How do we correctly understand this verse, which has been a go-to text on this issue for years? In fact, well-known pastors interpret it to support a husband/father leaving his wife and children for the gospel, even months and years at a time. Let us dive into this verse and ask God to show us his meaning.

Matthew 19:29 is parallel to Luke 18:29–30, except that Luke adds the noun "wife": "And He said to them, 'Truly, I say to you, there is no one who has left house or wife or brothers or parents or children, for the sake of the kingdom of God, who will not receive many times more in this time, and in the age to come eternal life'" (Luke 18:29–30).

Is it biblical for a missionary father/husband to always be gone for the kingdom of God to the point that his wife and children are alone, and his wife feels like a widow, and his children are being raised solely by their mother? Can we interpret these verses to support this belief? Is it acceptable to sacrifice the family unit for the kingdom of God?

Understanding the Context

First of all, we must understand the context of Matthew 19. It is easy to take a verse by itself and make it fit our own motives and interpretation, but I want to avoid that. We must approach this verse with a correct hermeneutic.[3] What is the context surrounding this verse?

In Matthew 19 (which I encourage you to read), we learn about a rich man who approaches Jesus and asks, "What good deed must I do to have eternal life" (v. 16)? This young man is genuinely seeking entrance into the kingdom of God. He wants to find the correct way to gain eternal life.

We know that the only way to enter the kingdom of God is through Christ alone, but this young man was wealthy and diligent in keeping the commandments. After all, he was brought up in Judaism, and when he comes to Jesus, he is seeking to add to what he thought was his already-perfect life to achieve an eternal place in God's kingdom. Knowing his heart, Jesus tells him to "keep the commandments" (v. 17). Jesus quotes half of the Ten Commandments as well as Leviticus 19:18. The young man is thrilled. You can imagine his smile as he answers Jesus, "All these I have kept. What do I still lack?" (v. 20). He could not have kept the commandments perfectly—no one can. In fact, James 2:10 says, "For whoever keeps the whole law but fails in one point has become guilty of all of it." But this man is convinced that he had obeyed these since his childhood.

---

3   "*Hermeneutics* comes from the Greek term, *hermeneuein*, which means to explain or interpret. In the Bible it is used in John 1:42; 9:7; Hebrews 7:2; and Luke 24:27. A noun formed from this verb, Hermes, was the name given to the Greek god who was the spokesman or interpreter for the other gods. The term 'hermeneutics,' which comes from these Greek words, simply describes the practice or discipline of interpretation." Robert H. Stein, *A Basic Guide to Interpreting the Bible: Playing by the Rules* (Grand Rapids: Baker Academic, 2011), 17.

He is also convinced that he still lacks something. Jesus cuts straight to his heart: "If you would be perfect, go, sell what you possess and give to the poor, and you will have treasure in heaven; and come, follow me" (v. 21). The phrase "follow me" is a present active imperative, meaning this command stresses a continual following. In effect, Jesus is saying, "The rest of your life is for me, and that means being my disciple, putting me first daily." This rich man was looking for something that could give him eternal life, but he was not expecting an ongoing, sacrificial following that would cost him his wealth and position. Verse 22 tells us that "he went away sorrowful, for he had great possessions." In the end, he cared more for his possessions, property, and self-interests than he did for obtaining salvation. The fact that he asked what he was lacking signified that he was ready to work for eternal life. But his response showed that he loved his possessions more than denying himself and following Christ.

In this story, we find the verse (Matt. 19:29) that is commonly used to justify someone—namely, the missionary husband/father, leaving his family for a long period of time for the sake of the gospel. But we cannot stop here and merely give an interpretation; the story continues. After the rich man leaves, Jesus turns to his disciples and says, "Truly, I say to you, only with difficulty will a rich person enter the kingdom of heaven. Again I tell you, it is easier for a camel to go through the eye of a needle than for a rich person to enter the kingdom of God" (vv. 23–24).

Understanding the Lesson

What is Jesus trying to teach his disciples from this statement? He wants them to pay close attention to what he is saying by using the common Jewish phrase, "Truly, I say to you" (v. 23). The wording "kingdom of heaven" (v. 23) and "kingdom of God" (v. 24) are parallel and represent eternal life, which is obtained through salvation. Jesus is teaching his disciples how difficult it is for a rich man to obtain eternal life.

As believers, we know that salvation is given freely through repentance of sin and faith in the Lord Jesus Christ. But Jesus, knowing the rich man's heart and seeing his love for his possessions and position, tells the disciples that it is impossible for one to gain eternal life without a willingness to lose everything. There must be a desire—which only comes from God—to forsake our sin and trust in Christ for forgiveness. This rich man could not let go of his sinful life, which entailed him worshiping his possessions instead of God.

That is what this passage is about. It is why Jesus uses the example of a camel going through the eye of a needle. In Jewish culture, this phrase is a normal way of expressing the impossibility of something. It is totally impossible for someone to let go of their sin without the regenerative work of God. John MacArthur writes, "This expression ... was a Jewish colloquialism for the impossible. It was probably a modified form of a Persian expression for impossibility, "easier for an elephant to go through the eye of a needle," that is quoted in the Talmud. Being the largest animal known in Palestine, the camel was substituted for the elephant."[4]

Is Jesus saying that a rich person has no way to obtain salvation? Not at all. The Holy Spirit can reach the most corrupt heart, whether rich or poor. Jesus is teaching his disciples that in and of themselves, possessions and great wealth are not bad, but if they place these things above Christ and believe in them for salvation or trust in them to work their way to heaven, then it is impossible to inherit eternal life. It is the same with us. It is impossible for us to keep God's law perfectly. We cannot obtain salvation this way. We cannot work our way to heaven by trusting in our wealth. Salvation is the treasure of eternal life. "For where your treasure is, there your heart will be also" (Matt. 6:21).

Amazed at this teaching, the disciples respond, "Who then can be saved" (v. 25)? Jesus answers, "With man this

4   John MacArthur, *Matthew 1–28*, MacArthur New Testament Commentary Four Volume Set (Chicago: Moody, 1989), 3:199.

is impossible, but with God all things are possible" (v. 26). A camel cannot go through the eye of a needle; neither can man work through his own means to gain eternal life. Both are impossible. Only God's regenerative work leads to eternal life. And because of who God is in his nature and character, it is possible for men to be saved. We are totally dependent on God's mercy as seen through the person and work of Christ Jesus for the forgiveness of sins. We only come to repentance and faith through the "all things are possible" way of God. We come to God only through God's way. And that way is to deny ourselves and give up everything and follow Christ.

Understanding the Application

At this point in the story, Peter is hopeful. He says to the Lord, "See, we have left everything [lit. "our own things"] and followed you. What then will we have" (v. 27)? He sees the difference in the disciples versus the rich man who walked away sorrowful. The disciples had already left everything and followed Jesus (Luke 5:11), they had been regenerated, and they believed that Jesus was the Son of God and that he had the "words of eternal life" (John 6:68). There was no sorrow for Peter and the other ten disciples (Judas excluded). They had forsaken everything to obtain saving faith and eternal life.

Notice his use of the word *followed*. He is showing Jesus they are truly his disciples; they have given up their sin and denied their wants and desires to follow him continually. The *Lexham Theological Wordbook* (LTW) says, "This word literally refers to following after someone physically. It is used this way in the NT (e.g., John 20:6). However, in the NT it is also sometimes used as a term for becoming a disciple (e.g., Matt. 9:9; Mark 1:18; Luke 5:11). These two concepts are not fully distinct; Jesus's disciples did in fact literally follow him around, but they also left behind their former lives to devote themselves fully to him."[5]

---

5   C. Byrley, "discipleship," *The Lexham Theological Wordbook*, edited by Douglas Mangum, et al. (Bellingham, WA: Lexham, 2014).

Did you catch what LTW said about Peter's word *follow?* It is "used as a term for becoming a disciple." This is important to remember as we answer the questions surrounding this passage, which is teaching about regeneration that is granted by God and not through means of man. When a person places his faith in Christ alone and follows him, that means he has forsaken his life of sin to be Christ's disciple, his follower.

Peter sincerely wants to know what they will receive. What is the reward? Jesus answers by saying, "Truly, I say to you, in the new world [regeneration, *palingenesia*], when the Son of Man will sit on his glorious throne, you who have followed me will also sit on twelve thrones, judging the twelve tribes of Israel" (v. 28). Spiritual regeneration happens in the hearts of men on this earth by God's power, and then one future day there will be a regeneration where Jesus Christ will sit on his throne and the disciples will take part in this regeneration. "Or do you not know that the saints will judge the world" (1 Cor. 6:2)? This is glorious news for believers now and when we "judge the world."

Keeping this in mind, let's look at another verse: "And everyone who has left houses or brothers or sisters or father or mother or children or lands, for my name's sake, will receive a hundredfold and will inherit eternal life" (v. 29). Now that we know the context of this passage and the lesson Jesus is giving, does this verse teach us that missionary husbands/fathers should sacrifice their families for gospel work? The answer is no. This verse is a response to the rich man's rejection of Christ. He would not give up his property for Christ's sake to receive forgiveness for his sins. Jesus is teaching his disciples that a person cannot place a higher value on worldly things and still expect to receive eternal life. But if a person leaves his house, family, possessions, or wealth to follow Christ in saving faith, he will receive eternal life.

J. C. Ryle said, "The Lord Jesus Christ shall be more to him than property, or relatives, or friends."[6] The crux of Matthew

---

6   J. C. Ryle, *Expository Thoughts on the Gospels: Luke, Vol. 2* (Carlisle, PA: Banner of Truth, 2012), 207.

19:29 speaks of salvation and what one must do to obtain it. It does not support leaving the family after one receives saving faith, as if God will be more pleased because of this "sacrifice." This verse teaches us that responding to the effectual call of the gospel that is freely offered will accompany, in different degrees, a forsaking of family, lands, possessions, wealth, relationships, and privileges—following Jesus always involves cost. Verse 29 specifically spells out the cost of following Christ in saving faith. We are already justified through his life, death, and resurrection; positionally, the Father cannot be more pleased with us than he already is through his Son. I know several believers who have left their families to follow Christ in saving faith. They abandoned their position, status, and religion to follow him in obedience. It cost them, sometimes even a violent cost. Although this verse speaks of "leaving" something to obtain something else, praise the Lord that as believers we are positionally sanctified and have his Spirit indwelling us now and forever.

The phrase Jesus uses, "will receive a hundredfold and will inherit eternal life," simply means that those who are regenerated will have every spiritual blessing in this life and for eternity. "Blessed be the God and Father of our Lord Jesus Christ, who has blessed us in Christ with every spiritual blessing in the heavenly places" (Eph. 1:3).

Many people who repent and believe experience the destruction of relationships because the cost of following Jesus is high. Christ calls people to be ready and willing to leave relationships for salvation. That salvation involves an ongoing following and commitment to Jesus Christ.

The belief that missionaries must leave their families for long periods of time for the gospel is unwarranted in this verse, and based on the texts discussed in the next section, it also is unbiblical.

Dear Missionary

My desire is to encourage you, especially husbands and fathers, to live a life on the mission field that communicates to your family that they are more important than your work. The crisis in missions is that some think they must "go for broke," meaning they believe God has sent them to do a huge task for the kingdom and they must do whatever it takes to have and show success in their ministry, even at the expense of their families.

Work hard in your mission endeavors, but do not to let them supersede your responsibilities to the family God has given you. Find a balance between work and family. Several missionaries have confessed to me that they are workaholics. They knew they worked too much, and it showed in their families.

On the field, it is easy to be caught up in your work from sunup to sundown. I have seen men work all day and never join their families for meals, play, or worship. During my first furlough, a wise friend counseled me when he noticed that I was not cutting off the work even after I went home. I was letting the tasks of writing, learning the tribal language, and helping others pursue missions infringe on family time. Praise the Lord that this man caught it and encouraged me because I did not see it. Today, I am more aware because of his instruction. I stop work at a certain time, and the rest is for my family.

For Patricia and me, our family comes first in our ministry but not to the point that we neglect our work. There must be a biblical balance. We should know ourselves well enough to find the times, especially on the field where we keep our own schedule, to work hard and to be with family. If we want healthy marriages that honor God and children who respect and obey us, we need to be in our home investing in them daily.

Missionary husbands and fathers must abandon the belief that God "needs" them in missions or ministry will not get done. What silliness this is. Missionary, do you understand this? God does not need you in cross-cultural missions. He chooses to use you, and despite your imperfections and weakness, he makes his name known through your foolishness of preaching and your sufferings. God is sovereign over all. He reigns supreme over his creation. How he chooses to save the lost does not provide us with an excuse to avoid the responsibilities he has given us as

the stresses and conflict they face, they need the body of Christ to walk with them. Your congregation must realize this is their ministry—you have sent the missionaries in your stead.

Furlough

Missionaries need rest. They will have to step away from the work for a season. The word *furlough* means a "'leave of absence,' especially in military use, 'leave or license given by a commanding officer to an officer or a soldier to be absent from service for a certain time,' from Dutch *verlof*, literally 'permission.'"[2] When most present-day churches hear this word, they automatically envision the missionary visiting churches to give a ministry report. Missionaries should report their work, bless and encourage their supporting churches, fan the flame for others to pursue full-time missions, and preach the Word and update the congregation in person about the work. But the church has taken the term *furlough* out of its original meaning.

Missionaries returning to the United States for any length of time need something from you before they start traveling to visit churches. They need rest, and they need you to tell them to rest. They should not sit around and become lazy, but they should put their work aside for several months and spend time with family, be fed through the Word, and fellowship with the congregation. Give them a place to come to so they can rest well. If you have the means, prepare comfortable accommodations for them. Counsel them to remain with you for at least two or three months to rejuvenate their bodies, hearts, and minds before visiting other churches. After a few weeks, allow them to update your congregation and encourage the congregation to ask what needs they have while stateside.

Your missionaries will face reentry culture shock. Do not expect them to be the same people they were before they left. They have been through battle; they have seen and experienced many intense trials in preaching the gospel. They will feel out of place and like they no longer belong at your church.

---

2   *Online Etymology Dictionary*, s.v. "furlough," accessed March 18, 2021, https://www.etymonline.com/word/furlough.

Things have changed for them. In the time they have been away, new people have come and people they knew have gone. The changes will be a lot for them to process. They will need quiet time with no visitors. One of the best things you as a church can do for your missionaries on furlough is to give them space, but at the same time, help to settle them for however long they stay.

Your missionaries might come back on furlough and fall sick with some disease or virus. After I had dengue fever, we traveled back to the States so I could heal. For six months, I spent most of my time in my room fighting severe depression and fatigue. I saw only a few supporters near the end of those six months. During our second furlough, we were not even two days in the States when I fell sick with *chikungunya* and then Guillain-Barré syndrome. My plans were quickly shattered, and I spent a year recovering. I could not see all my supporters because of sickness.

Churches, your missionaries want to visit you, but when they are sick and exhausted and need months or even years to recover, be understanding and let them know that you will continue to support them even if they cannot make it for a visit. Saying these words will encourage them more than you know and put them at ease, allowing them to more fully rest. A church that had supported me for a long time once emailed me to say they would no longer support us because we had not visited them for some time. They did not understand our position and situation. Although it is vital that missionaries visit their supporting churches, churches must understand the circumstances concerning missionary life. Sickness, lack of funds, depression, family trials, and other unavoidable setbacks can hinder missionaries from traveling. Churches can show love and support by reassuring the missionaries that they will continue to partner with and help them through these trials.

Finally, while on furlough your missionaries will need extra funding. They are not receiving large salaries. In fact, they have been living meagerly on the field. Once they are stateside, dental work and medical exams need to be updated, creating substantial bills. Travel expenses add up quickly while traveling to many churches. Think ahead for your missionaries and consider setting up a sub-account for furlough so they will be adequately supported when they visit.

After the Field

Sometimes God's sovereign plan for missionaries means they leave the field, whether after serving one year or twenty. Many missionaries must quit the mission field. Papua has one of the highest attrition rates in Indonesia because of its tropical diseases and geographical isolation. The stresses of everyday life are markedly pressing and can wear the body out quickly, causing an extended furlough or even permanent departure.

It is hard to leave the field. In fact, it will be one of the most difficult decisions a missionary will face. The sending church in such a situation needs to provide the missionaries wise counsel and compassionate understanding like never before. The decision to leave the field should be made together; as I said before, it is not just the missionary's ministry, it is the church's ministry. These decisions must be made together for the good of the missionary and the church. No missionary should come off the field unless his church tells him to or the church agrees with his decision.

What can cause a permanent departure from the field? Sickness, a child's well-being, emotional and mental problems in the family, marital problems, education for children, death of a spouse, death in the family, depression and mental fatigue, and sin. I have witnessed all of these. Each example quickly and drastically changes the lives of your missionaries, who foresaw a lifetime of service when they began. Some veteran missionaries may labor for thirty to fifty years before they are through. Either way, when a missionary comes off the field, you as a church need to be prepared for several difficulties.

Your missionaries may face depression, and it may be severe. Whether after several years or a lifetime, some missionaries will struggle to face their new life in the States with eagerness. For many years, they have made a different country their home, living their lives doing what they love for the Lord. To know that what they found joy in doing is over causes a roller coaster of emotions that may cast them down for a season. They have said goodbye to new believers and dear friends who they were teaching and discipling. They have left a work they loved dearly for Christ's name's sake, and now they must face the American church and try to put their feelings into words.

Most missionaries when coming off the field will not divulge everything they have experienced. They do not believe that anyone understands what they are going through. As loving and caring as your church may be, none of your members have experienced or will truly comprehend what your missionaries have been through. This situation is similar to soldiers returning from war with post-traumatic stress disorder. Depending on the field, it can be that severe. Your missionaries need to know that their church is there for them but without the pressure to share everything they are feeling. As a church, do not be silent; it is good for the elders to learn of their needs and help them as much as possible. When appropriate and after they have had time to decompress, personally and as a family, your mission-aries should debrief with the church leaders. At this point, the elders' job is to listen to them and love them. Make this a time of encouragement for their souls by giving them godly wisdom and counsel as needed. Simply listen. Ask what you can do for them, no matter what that might be.

If furlough sounded rough, transitioning back permanently is worse. Your missionaries feel like they do not belong any-where. They will likely experience a lengthy depression and need much prayer. They need an understanding church. They need financial support until they can find permanent work. Help your missionaries by writing to their supporting churches and requesting continued support until they have settled into permanent work. Make the transition back to the States as comfortable and easy as possible because there will be rough days ahead for your missionaries.

Many missionaries, including myself, deal with depression daily, even if they have not permanently left the field. Perhaps your missionaries need medical attention while dealing with reentry. I know of several who have struggled for years. Please be understanding and loving during these times.

Some mosquito viruses can leave severe mental side effects your missionaries will have to deal with daily. The dengue and chikungunya mosquitoes that infected me left me with no control over my mental state for several years. I still battle with mental problems, but thanks to the Lord's intervention, I received care and medicine from a doctor familiar with my condition and am now able to manage my symptoms. In this case, the mental ailments I am facing are not a spiritual problem but a lingering side effect of a virus that requires medical attention.

Yes, your missionaries need to consistently study the Word and pray so they do not fall into condemnation, but there may be, for a season, severe depression and mental fatigue that will not allow them to focus or even study. Encourage them and be there for them. Do not leave them alone in this regard but give them time to rest and let their minds find strength and comfort in the Lord Jesus, who will bring them through the dark days of weariness and restore their hearts and minds once more, perhaps not in the time frame we desire or expect, but in his perfect timing.

Father in heaven, thank you for the church, your sheep that you brought out of the mire and set on a rock as adopted sons and daughters. Thank you that you use us to bring in the lost sheep that you have chosen before the foundation of the world. Please send out more laborers to the unreached.

May each church be passionate about sending out missionaries so that your name would be great among the nations. Grant each church the opportunity to send missionaries to unreached peoples who are in darkness. Teach your people what it means

to send missionaries. Give churches clarity in their role as direct
senders. Help them to be understanding and loving in all areas
of missionary life. Show them how to wisely care for missionaries as they prepare to go, while they are on the field, and when
they return. May the relationship between the church and the
missionary be one that glorifies you and shows your worth to
the world.

May this be for the glory of your Son, Jesus Christ. Amen.

APPENDIX 1

Preaching the Gospel to a Remote People Group

In this appendix, I provide an example of how to preach the gospel to a people group that has not yet heard the name of Jesus. Specifically, this is how I preach the gospel to the tribes in the jungles of Papua, Indonesia.

The concept of time in the remote jungle is nonexistent, so I have written down a lengthy gospel history proclamation. Some opportunities will arise that call for shorter gospel preaching, so you can take from this and shorten it. Additionally, most interior people do not know how to read, so your language may call for more specific terms when preaching. This is in no way an exemplary way of preaching the gospel. Every messenger has his/her own unique preparation and style. This is only a simple example based on what I have written about the gospel in the previous pages.

Gospel Example Proclaiming Salvation History

Many years ago, before human beings were created, there was God. He was not created by anyone or anything but existed by himself.

There was no other god or powerful spirit; there was only God. He did not need anything or anyone. He is the most powerful being anywhere. He exists in three persons, the Father, the Son, and the Holy Spirit. They are three persons, but one God. We call this the Trinity, Three in One.

God the Father sent his Son to the earth as a man. He created everything through his Son. God the Son came as a man and died for evil, wicked, and sinful men. God the Holy Spirit was sent by the Father and the Son to show people their sin and live in each person who repents and believes.

This God is not like man. He is not like you and me. He is perfect. God does not sin, not even once. We sin. What is sin? We worship other spirits. We lie, steal, and murder. We commit adultery. We disobey our parents. We are jealous. We are selfish. We covet. Yet God never has nor ever will do any of these things. He cannot sin. He is holy. "Holy" means he does no wrong, and he is worthy of your worship. He lives in pure light where there is no darkness at all. He is sinless. God is also love.

What does it mean that God is love? God loves human beings so much that he sent his only Son to die in our place so we may live forever. That is true love. He is perfect. He is the most powerful person and controls everything. He is above everything you see. God owns everything in heaven and on earth. God created everything you see. He created light, water, rain, oceans and rivers, the land we live on, dirt, trees, rocks, plants, and fruit and vegetables. He created the sun, moon, and stars to give light day and night. He created all the animals, pigs, dogs, cows, lions, birds, lizards, spiders, insects, and fish. God created everything in six days. On the seventh day, he rested. God did not need to rest. He never gets tired. He rested from his work to make a special day. This special day was to be holy. This day was to be for worshiping him and resting from our work. When God looked at everything he had made, he said it was good. He was happy with everything he had made.

God also made man in his own image. He called the first man *Adam*. God made man to worship him and to work and take care of the earth. He made Adam from the dust of the ground. God put Adam in a garden full of food and water and everything he needed. Adam even named all the animals. Adam worshiped God in the garden. Everything was perfect and beautiful. Adam lived with God in the garden where everything was happy and sinless.

In the garden, there was a tree called "the tree of the knowledge of good and evil" (Gen. 2:9). God commanded Adam, "you shall not eat [of it], for in the day that you eat of it you shall surely die" (Gen. 2:17). Adam could eat from all the other trees in the garden, but not this one tree.

Then, God made woman from Adam's rib to help him. Adam called her *Eve*. Adam and Eve were the first man and woman, and they lived in the garden together as husband and wife. They are our grandparents. All human beings are from Adam and Eve. They lived with God in a beautiful garden with no sin, and they were created without sin.

One day, the enemy of God, who is Satan, came to Eve in the form of a serpent. Satan is evil. He hates God, who is all-powerful, all-knowing, and holy, without sin. Satan is jealous of God and wanted to be more powerful than God. Satan is a liar. He tempted Eve to eat the fruit that God told Adam not to eat. Satan told Eve, "You will not surely die. For God knows that when you eat of it your eyes will be opened, and you will be like God" (Gen. 3:4–5). Satan tempted Eve to disobey God's law. Eve looked and "saw that the tree was good for food, and that it was a delight to the eyes" (Gen. 3:6). She wanted it so much and saw that it was beautiful, so she ate the fruit God told her not to eat. She disobeyed God's command.

Then Eve gave the fruit to her husband, Adam, and he ate it. They both broke God's command. Immediately, they knew they were naked. They ran and hid from God because they knew they had sinned against the holy God.

Because Adam and Eve ate the fruit God told them not to, they became sinners, and the punishment for sin is death. That is why all people die because we have inherited Adam's sin. Adam and Eve would die, but God did not kill them right then. He covered their naked bodies and cast them out of the garden. No longer could they enjoy the beautiful garden where they would eat of its food and walk with God. Now Adam would have to work hard. He would become tired and sweat from his work. The ground would be hard to grow food. Eve would have pain in childbirth. They would suffer in life because of their sin against God. God did not kill them when they sinned even though he had every right to.

Adam and Eve had two sons. They called the first son Cain and the second son Abel. Cain and Abel were born with sinful, evil hearts because of their parents' sin. Cain became angry and jealous of his brother Abel's offering to the Lord, and Cain killed Abel. This was the first murder. Maybe you have murdered someone. If you have, you have disobeyed God's law. And the punishment for disobedience to God is death. God punished Cain by sending him away to roam the earth.

Adam and Eve had other sons and daughters. They had a son called Seth. Eve hoped Seth would save them from sin's curse, but he did not. The generations of Adam grew, and many offspring were born. The earth began to be filled with many people and tribes. People were evil, cruel, and wicked. They sinned before God and did not worship him as he commanded. The Lord saw man's wickedness and was sad that he had made man on the earth (Gen. 6:6). Humans did not care about God. They loved themselves more than him. They worshiped other gods. You too worship other spirits. You too have disobeyed God's law. God said he would erase man, animals, and birds because he was sorry he had made them.

One of Adam's descendants was named Noah. Noah's father thought his son would save them from sin's curse. But Noah was not the savior. However, Noah was a worshiper of God. He wanted to serve God and do what was right. God blessed Noah and his family and told Noah to build an ark. God was going to kill everyone on earth and all the animals.

God sent a flood that covered the whole earth, but first God took Noah and his family with two of every kind of animal inside the ark, male and female. Then God closed the door of the ark and sent the flood to kill mankind. Rain fell on the earth forty days and nights. Water burst out from under the earth. Everyone died because of their wickedness. But God saved Noah, his wife, their three sons, and their wives.

God kept his promise to Noah and his family. After 150 days, the rain stopped, and the water receded. God made dry land appear and Noah and his family went out of the ark. Noah worshiped God and made an altar where he sacrificed an offering to God. God made a rainbow in the clouds. This was a promise that God would never flood the earth again. Noah's three sons were Shem, Ham, and Japheth. All the tribes of the earth are from Shem, Ham, and Japheth. Years later the generations of Noah's sons were many. But people were still evil and haters of God. They worshiped other spirits and did not worship God as he commanded. From the generations of Noah's sons, Ham, Shem, and Japheth, came a people that did not listen to the Lord God. They had one language and lived in one place. But the Lord God came to them and confused their language so that they spoke different languages. Then God scattered the people across the whole earth. This is the reason there are so many languages today.

One of Shem's descendants was Abram. God told Abram, "You will become a great nation. From you all the earth will be blessed" (Gen. 12:2, paraphrased). Abraham would be the father of many nations. What did God mean? He meant that Jesus Christ, his Son, would come from the family of Abraham and save many people from their sin. If a person follows Jesus Christ, they are in Abraham's family. From Abram and his wife, Sarai, would come their Savior who would save them from sin and death.

Abram obeyed God's word and commands. But Abram and Sarai had no son. How would Abram become a great nation without a son? God told Abraham he would have a son in his old age. And then Sarah gave birth to their first son at age ninety-nine; his name was Isaac. From Isaac, the generations of Abraham multiplied. Isaac married Rebekah, and she gave birth to Esau and Jacob. God chose Jacob over Esau to receive a blessing from his father. From Jacob came the twelve tribes of Israel. These people would be the chosen nation of God. Of all other nations, they would be God's special people. One of the twelve tribes of Israel was called Judah, and from this tribe would come a savior, Jesus Christ, the Son of God, to save his people from their sin.

The nation of Israel grew strong and large, but the nation of Egypt forced the Israelites to work hard and suffer under an evil king named Pharaoh. Pharaoh was wicked and wanted all the Israelite sons that were born to be killed so that Israel would not continue to grow strong. But God was loving to his nation. A male Israelite baby was born whose name was Moses. God chose Moses to lead the people of Israel out of Egypt, away from their enemy.

For many years, the Israelites suffered in Egypt, but God did not forget the promise he made to Abraham, that he would become a great nation. God used Moses to warn Pharaoh to let his people go, but Pharaoh would not listen, even after God sent nine plagues. God then commanded Moses, his brother Aaron, and the people of Israel to kill a lamb and place the blood on the sides and top of their doors because God would send an angel to come and kill each firstborn child in Egypt. The blood on the doors would keep them safe. The angel of God came that night, but God saved his people. When the angel saw the blood on each door, he passed by that house. If there was no blood on the door, the angel went in and killed the firstborn child. After this, Pharaoh let the people of Israel go. God saved his people from their enemies. God saved his people with the blood of a lamb on a door, and many years later, Jesus, God's Son, would have his blood spilled on a cross to rescue sinners like you and me.

Moses led the people of Israel into the desert, and the Lord led his people with a cloud in the day and with fire at night. Pharaoh was angry that he let the people go, so he sent soldiers after them. When the Israelites saw the soldiers, they became afraid and were mad at Moses for bringing them into the desert to die. But God would not forget his people. Moses stretched out his hand over the sea and God parted the waters so that the Israelites could escape. The water became two walls. The land between the walls was dry, and the people of Israel passed through the water. Once again God saved his people. When the Israelites were through to the other side, Moses stretched out his hand over the sea again and the water closed in over the Egyptian soldiers. All the soldiers drowned. God protected his people.

When the people of Israel were in the desert, God promised them a new land for their inheritance. They came to the mountain of Sinai, and God met with Moses on this mountain, but he forbade anyone else from touching the mountain or going up. If anyone touched the mountain, they would die because God was there. Sinful man cannot be where God is because God is holy and righteous. The Lord God allowed Moses to go up the mountain to speak with him. Moses wanted to see the glory of God on this mountain, but no one can see God's face and live. God was kind to Moses and shielded him with his hand, while Moses stood in an opening in a rock. Moses was able to see God's back after God passed by him. Then, the Lord gave the people of Israel Ten Commandments to obey:

1. You shall have no other gods before me.
2. You shall not make a carved image and bow down or serve that image.
3. You shall not take the name of the Lord your God in vain.
4. Remember the Sabbath day to keep it holy.
5. Honor your father and mother.

6. You shall not murder.
7. You shall not commit adultery.
8. You shall not steal.
9. You shall not lie (bear false witness against your neighbor).
10. You shall not covet your neighbor's house, his wife, his servants, his animals, or anything that is your neighbor's.

We have broken all these commandments. God's law shows us that we are sinners. That means we are all guilty before God. God said, "if you have broken one of these, you have broken all of them" (James 2:10, paraphrased). Who has stolen something? Who has lied? We all have. We have disobeyed God's law, and that is called sin. Because we have disobeyed God's law, we are punished with death. We are separated from God. He cannot be in the presence of sin. This law was given to the people of Israel to show them what sin is. Only one person in all the world has kept God's law perfectly, and that is Jesus Christ, the Son of God. We were made to worship and obey God and to love one another—not to beat our wives; murder when we are mad; steal other people's possessions; or worship rocks, trees, water, plants, or evil spirits. We were made to worship and love the Lord God. This is the greatest commandment: "Love the LORD your God with all your heart and with all your soul and with all your might" (Deut. 6:5).

After God's law was given to the people of Israel, they forgot him and his word and broke his commandments. They worshiped other gods. They committed adultery. The punishment for these things was death. Because of Israel's sin, they were made to wander in the desert for forty years.

But God did not forget his people. Because he is so holy and pure, he told the people to make a tent in which he could come down and dwell with them. The people of Israel would bring animals to sacrifice to God for the forgiveness of their sin. Moses's brother, Aaron, would go into the Holy Place inside the tent and offer an animal for the people's sins. This happened every year. Blood had to be shed for the forgiveness of sin. God promised them a new land, named Canaan, where they could live and worship him.

Eventually Moses died, and God replaced him with Joshua to lead his people. Joshua was a man of God and led the people into the promised land, but first they had to cleanse the land of all their enemies. Once they had victory over their enemies in the land, Joshua said, "Choose this day whom you will serve." The people responded, "Therefore we also will serve the LORD, for he is our God" (Josh. 24:15, 18).

Then Joshua died. Many years passed, and the people of Israel sinned again against the Lord. They forgot him and worshiped and bowed down to idols like Baal. Because of this sin, God sent Israel's enemies to kill them, but he did not forget his people because of his promise to Abraham.

God chose a man named Gideon to destroy Israel's enemies and the idols that they made and worshiped. Gideon was weak and afraid, but God was with him. God used this weak man to bring his people back to him. This is the way God works. He uses men and women who are weak and have no strength in themselves.

Again, the Israelites worshiped other gods, the Lord raised up a man named Samuel, and the Lord sent Samuel to judge them for their sin. God delivered them from their enemies, but again, they rejected him by asking for a king to rule over them. God gave them a king whose name was Saul. But Saul sinned against God by not obeying his commands. God took the kingdom away from him.

The generations of Israel continued to disobey and forget God. He did not forget them because of his promise to Abraham, but he gave them a new king whose name was David. David worshiped and feared God. As king, David lived in the city of Jerusalem. He ruled over the city and the people. The people of Israel had many enemies. King David, by God's power, defeated the enemies of Israel. David was a man of war who had shed much blood in battle. David longed to build a temple for God so that God would no longer have to dwell with his people from a tent. Because David had shed much blood in war, God told David his son would one day build the temple. David trusted the word of the Lord in this matter. Even though David was a man who feared God, David sinned against God by committing adultery with a woman. Her name was Bathsheba. She became pregnant, and David tried to hide this sin and pregnancy from Bathsheba's husband, Uriah. David had Uriah killed in battle to cover up his sin and the plans for Bathsheba. God punished David through the death of his son. King David repented of his sin, and God gave him another son. His name was Solomon. God used Solomon to build a temple, the house of the Lord God. He would no longer dwell in a tent like in the desert. Instead, he would enter this new temple and meet with his people. The Israelites would offer sacrifices to God. Blood would be shed at the temple, and they would come to be forgiven of their sins.

Today, people who follow Jesus Christ are the temple of God because the Holy Spirit makes his home in us. This building we worship in is just wood. It will rot, but people who follow Jesus will live forever. No longer must we sacrifice animals to be forgiven of sins. Jesus, the Son of God, was the final sacrifice for sins. No longer does God fill just a building with his Spirit. Christians are filled with his Spirit. They are the house of God. But this story has more sad news.

Again, the people of Israel forgot the Lord and did not worship him. God sent prophets like Isaiah and Jeremiah to Israel. These prophets warned them to repent and turn back to God or he would punish them. But they would not listen, so God sent judgment once again. Their enemy, the nation of Babylon, came and destroyed Jerusalem and took the people as slaves. God punished them for their sin, and they were slaves to another nation. They suffered in Babylon, but God did not forget his promise to Abraham. He remembered his people and brought them back to Jerusalem after seventy years of suffering. A man named Nehemiah rebuilt the walls of Jerusalem, and a man named Ezra opened the Word of God and read to all the people of Israel and they repented of their sins against God. But the people of Israel would again worship other gods.

Around four hundred years later, the promise God made with Abraham appeared. Remember, the promise was, "And I will make of you a great nation, and I will bless you and make your name great, so that you will be a blessing. I will bless those who bless you, and him who dishonors you I will curse, and in you all the families of the earth shall be blessed" (Gen. 12:2–3). How would they be blessed? They would be saved from sin and death through the Messiah.

Great news: The Messiah, Jesus Christ, has come. For thousands of years, people had looked for Jesus Christ. He had finally come as a man to die for sinners. God had come in flesh. Through this Messiah, Abraham would become a great nation.

God the Father sent his only Son, Jesus, to be born of a virgin named Mary. Mary did not know a man. She did not know her husband Joseph until after Jesus was born. Jesus left his home in heaven with his Father and became a human being. He had skin like ours. He had a body like ours; yet he was truly God and truly man together. Jesus is God, yet he was born in a place where animals were kept. This King of the world was not born in a palace. He was not rich; he was poor. He had no possessions; he was not surrounded with gold. He did not have an army; he was simply the son of two poor Jews.

Jesus grew to become a wise young boy, a wise teenager, and full of wisdom as an adult. He never once disobeyed his parents. He never lied, stole, treated his mother and father badly, murdered, had a jealous thought, or had a selfish desire. He was holy like his Father. He was perfect. He never sinned. He was tempted to sin, like we are, but he never sinned.

Jesus proved that he was the Son of God through his ministry. He chose twelve men to become his disciples. He trained these men to teach and lead his people. They learned who Jesus was and how to preach the good news. During Jesus's ministry, through the power of the Holy Spirit, he raised the dead and healed the lame, blind, deaf, and the leper. No one can count how many people Jesus healed. This proved that he was God in the flesh. Everywhere Jesus went to heal, he also preached the good news of the kingdom of God. The good news is that God came as a man, this man is Jesus, and he will save his people from their sin. Jesus commanded people to repent and believe in him. Just like the Israelites were commanded, Jesus commanded his people to return to God the Father and to repent of their sin against God. We have all broken God's law; therefore, we deserve death and hell, but Jesus can forgive our sin if we repent and follow him as Lord and Savior. He can give us new life. Even though we sit here and breathe, we are dead spiritually because of our sin. Jesus is the only one who can give us new life that is eternal.

But you must follow a command: You must repent of your sin and believe by faith the work that Jesus accomplished on the cross. What is repentance? Repentance is simply a change of mind. Right now, you are serving and following the devil. You are a slave to him. But when you repent of sin, you change your direction and go the opposite way, the way that leads to Christ. You want to be a slave to Jesus and follow him. That is repentance.

Jesus suffered greatly because many of his own people tried to kill him. They rejected him and hated him. They did not want to believe his words that he was the way, the truth, and the life and that no one comes to the Father but through him (John 14:6). Jesus is the only way to God the Father. He is eternal life. Jesus came to this earth for one reason: to die a painful death on a tree and bear the sin of sinful people like you and me. He was beaten, mocked, spit on, and a crown of thorns was pushed into his head. He was whipped until you could not recognize him. He suffered greatly for sinners. Then, he was hung on the cross in shame. He was nailed to the tree where he hung gasping for every breath. Jesus, the Holy Son of God, did this so that sinners, like you and me, may truly live and worship him. God the Father placed all the sin of all those who will believe on Jesus.

But the good news does not end there. When sinners repent and believe, Jesus gives them something. He gives the repentant heart his righteousness. He took our sin, and we receive his righteousness. Jesus is righteousness because he is God and cannot sin. The repentant person receives his Spirit to live in him. Now, the Father looks at that person as he looks at his Son Jesus. God the Father declares that we are righteous and are made clean, but that only happens through repentance. Jesus died in the place of sinners. He suffered and satisfied the wrath of his Father. We deserve to suffer what happened to Jesus. We deserve death and hell. But Jesus suffered all that for us. There had to be a sacrifice, a shedding of blood for sin. Jesus was that sacrifice for sinners. In the Old Testament, before Jesus's sacrifice on the cross, they sacrificed animals, and blood had to be shed over and over. The sacrifice of animals was not enough to destroy sin forever. But Jesus sacrificed himself one time for sinners so that we could return to the Father and have everlasting life. The sacrifice of Jesus was perfect—perfect enough to destroy sin forever. Jesus's Father accepted his Son's sacrifice on the cross and gave his Son a reward for his work. That reward is all the people who repent of their sin and believe in Jesus's name. God is angry with sinners every day, but God is also love. He loves sinners like you and me, and through his Son Jesus, we can know this love by repenting of our sin and believing in Jesus alone. We cannot work our way to God. We cannot come to a place of worship and think that is enough. We cannot help other people and think that is enough. Nothing will save us but Jesus. If we do not repent and believe in Jesus alone, we will suffer forever in a place of darkness and fire called hell. This is where the enemies of God are placed where they will suffer forever and ever.

After Jesus died on the cross, he was laid in a tomb. He rose from the grave three days later. He was dead, and now he is alive. Have you ever seen a person buried come back to life? No, but Jesus did. He has the power over death. He has the power over sin. Jesus came "to destroy the works of the devil" (1 John 3:8). The devil does not want you to believe this. Your flesh does not want to believe this. But God's Word says this happened. If you believe by faith that this is true, and confess your sins, God the Father will cleanse you from your sin and give you true life. Once Jesus was resurrected from the grave, he showed himself to five hundred people, proving that he was indeed alive.

Jesus spent time with his disciples and friends, commanding them to teach others also. They were to preach this good news so other people, like you and me, could have the forgiveness of sins and worship God with a pure heart. Jesus promised to send his Holy Spirit to live in each believer. The Holy Spirit would now make his home in each person who repents and believes. No longer would God just dwell in a temple. Believers in Jesus would become his temple. How do you know if you are a Christian? A true Christian does not want to sin against God. A true Christian wants to please God and obey his Word and follow him in obedience. A true Christian will show God's love to others.

In front of many witnesses, Jesus ascended to his Father where he is to this day. After Jesus returned to his Father, one of his disciples named Peter preached the good news of Jesus (his life, death, and resurrection) to many people. More than three thousand people repented of their sin and believed in Jesus. This started the first church. The believers would gather and be taught God's Word, pray (thanking God for his Son, asking him to provide their needs), and eat and drink together, remembering Jesus's death. They helped one another, gave to the poor, and preached the good news to sinners. This was the first church in Jerusalem.

Jesus promised that he would return someday. Christians are waiting eagerly for his return to take us to his home, heaven. While we wait, we are commanded through his Word to love him with all our heart, soul, strength, and mind, and to love our neighbors as ourselves (Luke 10:27). Do you obey this command?

Repent and believe in Jesus alone for the forgiveness of sins. Today is the day of salvation.

APPENDIX 2

My Testimony of Conversion

Growing up, I was surrounded by religious activity. I was a PK and an MK—a preacher's kid and a missionary's kid. My whole life was religion.

And yet I was an unsaved hypocrite.

What is a hypocrite? I know this definition better than most because I lived every essence of the word. A hypocrite is someone who focuses on external appearances but does not desire his soul to be clean within; who trusts in his outward actions, even in a congratulatory manner, as a way to commend himself before God; whose feet actions do not reflect his mouth claims; who convinces himself he is bound for heaven but in reality is dangling over the fire and at any moment could drop into everlasting torment.

I was the son of a pastor, the son of a missionary. No one questioned my supposed allegiance to God—not even myself—because I owned the religious titles. I lived on the mission field, I played with other pastors' kids, I spent my life in church, I knew all the terminology, I knew how to behave in the presence of polite company.

And yet I was an unsaved hypocrite.

Year after year, I sat through church services believing all was well with my soul, singing, "Oh, how I love Jesus,"[1] and then I would walk out the doors and live like the devil. I possessed head knowledge while lacking heart transformation. My "repentance" was a mirage. Trusting in a momentary prayer feigning repentance is not the same as trusting in the God who grants a lifestyle of repentance. My lifestyle, in contrast, showed who I really was. I stiff-armed God in the face while mouthing my love for him. John the Baptist said, "Bear fruit in keeping with repentance" (Matt. 3:8), but there was no fruit in my life that backed up who I claimed to be.

When I was twenty-six, I suffered a rodeo injury. Healing was a difficult process, and I found myself doing a lot of spiritual wrestling. God found me and opened my eyes when I was not looking for him. He found me spiritually dead in my sins one evening while I was listening to the preaching of the gospel. The condition of my heart was exposed by the light and beauty of his Word. He caused me to see my need for him and that he stood before me with his arms open, freely offering this wicked sinner the forgiveness of sins. He granted repentance to me, even after I had accrued such a weight of sin. For the first time in my life, I saw my sin and his perfect holiness. I remember weeping with such joy over the forgiveness that he granted me because I did not have to hide anything anymore. I was free, and the saving faith that God gave me fell upon my soul in such a way that I could not refuse his grace. True repentance takes place only through the work of the Spirit of Christ in one's life. This true repentance began to affect my everyday life. It had feet, and it began to mobilize me for action.

Maybe you are also sitting in church even while you are under the wrath of God. Maybe you are performing religious exercises, and yet your soul is black. Maybe you are doing well at "playing church" on Sunday mornings and putting on the mask that would reveal your true identity should it slip. Perhaps this mask hides your lack of love for God's Word and

---

1   Frederick Whitfield, "Oh, How I Love Jesus" (1855).

your lack of respect for God in your Monday-through-Saturday lifestyle. Maybe you are a deacon's kid, a preacher's kid, or a lifelong church member but are trusting in these labels and not realizing your lost state.

And you too are an unsaved hypocrite.

How much greater will your damnation be on the day of judgment if you sin against such a holy and infinite God? It will be better for the unreached tribes of Papua, Indonesia, that sit in darkness than it will be for your soul.

Repent therefore, and turn back, that your sins may be blotted out. (Acts 3:19)

How I thank my God that he saw fit to save me and to save me with the purpose of service as a missionary like my father. My wife, Trish, and I serve in the remotest place on earth, ministering to a tribe in the lowland swamps of Papua, the Korowai. Indonesia is not too distant from my childhood home of Australia. Although I left Australia as an unsaved man and self-serving hypocrite, I have come to Asia as a saved man who God called into his divine service to pour out my life so others may taste the sweet wine of his mercy.

Praise God for that mercy! Praise God that although my obstinacy hardened my heart as packed clay, God in his mercy softened it with his love. And now, I even rejoice that God may use my story of hypocrisy amid a life of religious activities to awaken you to your sin and cause you to seek the true God who is not content to merely polish the exterior of the sepulchre but desires to make you whole within.

> Here am I, send me; send me to the ends of the earth; send me to the rough, the savage pagans of the wilderness; send me from all that is called comfort on earth; send me even to death itself, if it be but in Thy service, and to promote Thy kingdom.[2]

2   David Brainerd, *The Life and Diary of the Rev. David Brainerd with Notes and Reflections by Jonathan Edwards*, ed. Jonathan Edwards, Kindle edition (Cornerstone Classic Ebooks, June 4, 2013), 282.

Bibliography

à Brakel, Wilhelmus. *The Christian's Reasonable Service*. Vol. 1. Edited by Joel R. Beeke. Translated by Bartel Elshout. Grand Rapids: Reformation Heritage Books, 2015.

Alexander, James W. *Thoughts on Family Worship*, edited by Don Kistler. Grand Rapids: Soli Deo Gloria, 1998.

Arndt, William, Frederick W. Danker, Walter Bauer, and F. Wilbur Gingrich. *A Greek-English Lexicon of the New Testament and Other Early Christian Literature*. Chicago: University of Chicago Press, 1979.

Beeke, Joel R. *How Should Men Lead Their Families?* Grand Rapids: Reformation Heritage Books, 2014.

Brainerd, David. *The Life and Diary of the Rev. David Brainerd with Notes and Reflections by Jonathan Edwards*. Edited by Jonathan Edwards. Cornerstone Classic Ebooks, June 4, 2013. Kindle.

Bright, Bill. "Have You Heard of the Four Spiritual Laws?" CRU Press. https://crustore.org/catalog/product/view/id/918/s/4-spiritual-laws-english/category/150.

Brown, Scott T., and Jeff Pollard. *A Theology of the Family*. Wake Forest, NC: National Center for Family-Integrated Churches, 2014.

Coleman, Doug. *A Theological Analysis of the Insider Movement Paradigm from Four Perspectives: Theology of Religions, Revelation,*

Soteriology and Ecclesiology, Evangelical Missiological Society Dissertation Series. Pasadena, CA: William Carey International University Press, 2011.

Ferguson, Sinclair B. *Grow in Grace*. Carlisle, PA: Banner of Truth, 1989.

Grudem, Wayne A. *Systematic Theology: An Introduction to Biblical Doctrine*. Grand Rapids: Zondervan, 1994.

Hamilton, James M. Jr. *What Is Biblical Theology?: A Guide to the Bible's Story, Symbolism, and Patterns*. Wheaton, IL: Crossway, 2013.

Lawson, Steven J. *The Passionate Preaching of Martyn Lloyd-Jones*. Orlando: Reformation Trust, 2016.

MacArthur, John. *Alone with God: Rediscovering the Power and Passion of Prayer*. 3rd ed. Colorado Springs: David C. Cook, 2011.

———. *Matthew 1–28 MacArthur New Testament Commentary Four Volume Set*. Chicago: Moody, 1989.

———. "Praying Without Hypocrisy." Grace to You, October 21, 1979. https://www.gty.org/library/sermons-library/2230/praying-without-hypocrisy.

Mangum, Douglas, Derek R. Brown, Rachel Klippenstein, and Rebekah Hurst, eds. *The Lexham Theological Wordbook*. Logos Bible Software (Version 9.2). Bellingham, WA: Lexham Press, 2014.

Manser, Martin H., Alister E. McGrath, J. I. Packer, and Donald J. Wiseman, eds. *Zondervan Dictionary of Bible Themes: An Accessible and Comprehensive Tool for Topical Studies*. Logos Bible Software (Version 9.2). Grand Rapids: Zondervan, 1999.

McDonald, James, MA, MSc. "Medieval Torture." Medieval Warfare. Revised February 24, 2015, https://www.medievalwarfare.info/torture.htm#chair.

Murray, John. *O Death, Where Is Thy Sting?: Collected Sermons*. Philadelphia: Westminster Seminary Press, 2017.

Owen, John. *Works of John Owen, Vol. 6: Temptation and Sin*. Edited by William H. Goold. Carlisle, PA: Banner of Truth, 1966.

Paton, John G. *John G. Paton: Missionary to the New Hebrides. An Autobiography*. Edited by James Paton. Carlisle, PA: Banner of Truth, 1965.

Ryle, J. C. *Expository Thoughts on the Gospels: Luke*. Carlisle, PA: Banner of Truth, 2012.

Sills, M. David. *Reaching and Teaching: A Call to Great Commission Obedience*. New ed. Chicago: Moody, 2010.

Sitton, David. *Reckless Abandon: A Modern-Day Gospel Pioneer's Exploits Among the Most Difficult to Reach Peoples*. Greenville, SC: Ambassador International, 2011.

Sproul, R. C. "Questions & Answers." Standing Firm: 2012 West Coast Conference. Sanford, FL: Ligonier Ministries. 2012. http://www.ligonier.org/learn/conferences/standing-firm-2012-west-conference/questions-and-answers-west-conference/.

———. *The Work of Christ: What the Events of Jesus' Life Mean for You*. 1st ed. Colorado Springs: David C. Cook, 2012.

Spurgeon, Charles Haddon. "The Throne of Grace." In The Metropolitan Tabernacle Pulpit Sermons, Vol. 17. London: Passmore & Alabaster, 1871.

Stein, Robert H. *A Basic Guide to Interpreting the Bible: Playing by the Rules*. 2nd ed. Grand Rapids: Baker Academic, 2011.

Vanderkooi, Mary. *The Village Medical Manual: A Layman's Guide to Health Care in Developing Countries*. 6th ed. Pasadena, CA: William Carey Library, 2009.

Ware, Bruce A. *The Man Christ Jesus: Theological Reflections on the Humanity of Christ*. Wheaton, IL: Crossway, 2013.

Washer, Paul. *The Gospel of Jesus Christ.* Grand Rapids: Reformation
Heritage Books, 2016.

———. *Ten Indictments against the Modern Church*, Reformation Today
Series. Grand Rapids: Reformation Heritage Books, 2018.

Wilson, Jared C. *Gospel Wakefulness.* Wheaton, IL: Crossway, 2011.

Wood, D. R. W., I. H. Marshall, A. R. Millard, J. I. Packer, and D.
J. Wiseman, eds. *New Bible Dictionary.* 3rd ed. Logos Bible
Software (Version 9.2). Downers Grove, IL: InterVarsity
Press, 2004.